Mr. C's Digest— What a cool trip

Moments of Mayhem, Memory,

Music and Murder

LARRY COOPER

iUniverse, Inc.

Bloomington

Mr. C's Digest—What a cool trip
Moments of Mayhem, Memory, Music and Murder

iUniverse books may be ordered through booksellers or by contacting:

iUniverse
1663 Liberty Drive
Bloomington, IN 47403
www.iuniverse.com
1-800-Authors (1-800-288-4677)

ISBN: 978-1-4759-3219-5 (sc)
ISBN: 978-1-4759-3220-1 (ebk)

Printed in the United States of America

iUniverse rev. date: 06/16/2012

Chapter One

The Dance

I t was the summer of 1955. A few months before my mother divorced my father and remarried in California. Each Friday evening during the summer a free dance was held outside of one of the two radio stations serving my hometown in northern Colorado. Teens were invited to come dance because beginning at 7 p.m. the station would play new records and the broadcast could be heard through speakers mounted on the wall.

There was a live radio broadcast underway and a few teenagers had gathered on a platform located adjacent to the radio station. Boys together on one side, girls together on the other glancing nervously at one another across a makeshift wooden plank dance floor. The announcer inside was taking phone calls from listeners and was urging the visitors outside to dance with one another, that is girl-boy—boy girl—"get brave kids get together—you might like it!" he kept repeating.

You could see the announcer if you peeked through a window adjacent to the dance floor. The Disc Jockey was a balding middle-aged man who was in fact the station's chief engineer. He'd use as a theme song (Theme songs were used in those days as a program and "personality" identifier) a Dixieland version of the *Muskrat Ramble* and he would repetitively urge more listeners to "come on out and join the fun!" As the evening darkness gradually settled in, the red glow from big 6 foot neon letters mounted on the broadcast tower provided the only light.

That was my first exposure to broadcasting. Each Friday night that summer I showed up for the program not to dance I was too shy for that, but to watch the D.J. who would open the studio door for me to get into the building. I learned to operate the control board by watching him work.

Part of the reason to write this book is to share some thoughts on lessons learned from my diverse career and life experiences that readers might find useful or at least of interest. *The Dance* represents my belief that you often must create your own opportunities by demonstrating your individual strengths and in order to do that you must focus on creating opportunities that clearly lend themselves to those traits.

When I attended Middle School, a buddy and I decided to write our own version of a tabloid. We called it *The Hot Sheet*. Even then I had a vague sense I wanted to be a reporter. We wrote a two pager each week about school activities complete with a gossip section identifying what boys liked what girls and vice versa. We would make copies on a rough mimeograph copier the school owned.

When I left a copy of this *Hot Sheet* lying on a table in the radio station's control room the station's manager took notice. A few days later I was asked if I would consider putting together a little fifteen minute radio broadcast on Saturday mornings, reading stories from my "Hot Sheet" and playing songs my friends might like. I said yes and one Saturday morning I awkwardly and nervously did my first broadcast. Because I could type with some skill and the *Hot Sheet* suggested I might have basic writing skills, I was asked to try writing a commercial. I did, the manager liked it and soon I was working at *a typewriter*.

For the enlightenment of younger readers a *typewriter* is a mechanical device allowing you to imprint letters on a page by beating on lettered keys, kind of a word processor without computer chips. I worked after school for an hour or so each day writing commercials.

The engineer sent a letter off to the Federal Communications Commission to get me a license that would technically allow me to write down required hourly transmitter readings. The announcer on duty was required by law to write down transmitter gauge readings to ensure the station's signal didn't surpass its allotted strength, didn't interfere with the signals from other stations and/or shift your location on the dial.

I found myself agreeing to work on Saturday afternoons operating the control board, not announcing anything other than the station call letters and town location. I was paid seventy-five cents an hour. I thought that was a great deal. My mentor was happy as well for he could spend his Saturday working on the equipment and not worrying about keeping the programs going. One of my tasks was to "engineer" a weekly live broadcast in the studio featuring Adolph Lesser's accordion students. Adolph and his wife operated a music store for many years and led a popular local polka band. Adolph was considered "the Polka Master" and his band was nationally recognized. Adolph first started radio broadcasts in the 1930s.

When I was fifteen my voice started to change allowing me to lower my voice while hoping against hope that my voice didn't crack. I was allowed to read on the air. I was to host a regular music program working as needed, usually on Saturday afternoons and Sunday mornings. Sunday involved putting the weekly live remote feed of local church services on the air.

When I entered ninth grade (1956) rock n' roll was just beginning to pick up popularity but in our conservative 1950s town most of those over thirty years of age wrote off the new music as "bar blues." Many believed Elvis was African American, until the world saw him move on the Ed Sullivan Television Show. To locals that music was only to be played at the "just over the city limits" bars.

Blues and soul bands were hired at those establishments because the performers could pick up a few extra bucks before hitting nearby Denver. I wasn't old enough to get in the door to listen, but I would walk over there and stand outside the front door just listening to the music. Another early life lesson; seek acceptable alternatives whenever feasible. Nonetheless the impact of rock and roll could not be ignored so the Friday night program eventually became a teenage request show and expanded to five nights a week. That same year I was asked to be the DJ for that teen-age request show because I was in fact a teenager. By my senior year in high school, I was getting so many song requests at night the manager hired a young lady to join me to handle phones and write down all the requests.

Compared to today's very targeted, formula-driven radio there was a simplicity then that was fun and honest and not really meant to accomplish much more than attract and entertain. Looking back now, it was great fun; the songs were fun and simple, no innuendos, no vulgarity just fun. Sometimes I'd read twenty or thirty "from and to" names per song and the kids loved it. By way of example, I would get a dedication request from a guy who sat by a cute girl in class but was too shy to speak to her. In the course of the evening she was sending songs to him. By the end of the program they would be "hooking up" but the next night the request would change to a song with lyrics like "Breaking up is Hard to do." Friday and Saturday night shows were the most fun because teens gathered on the main street to drive up and down the street, with radios blaring, waving and shouting. We called it "cruising."

Late at night when I would arrive home I would quietly get ready for bed trying not to awaken my Dad, sneaking my battery-powered radio beneath my blankets to listen to "Wolf Man Jack" on a distant 50,000 watt radio station. That (listening to tunes in bed), I suppose is easier today with ear-buds and tiny players loaded with thousands of songs. In the 50s that would have been something like Dick Tracy's then fictional wrist watch. It is remarkable to listen to thousands of songs on a very small little digital device you can carry anywhere. In many ways though it is sad for what's missing now is the connection with a local disc jockey. As Wolf Man Jack put it in an interview recorded with him before his death "Computers have no soul." Unfortunately Wolf Man Jack passed away in the mid-90s.

By the time I was a junior in High School I was preparing and reading news broadcasts, taking regular on-air shifts and actually selecting all the music to be broadcast. I would make frequent trips to record warehouses in nearby Denver. The station manager would hand me $20 in cash. For that I could select about thirty albums to take back to work to put into the station's music format. I actually reformatted the music for the entire broadcast day. We programmed to the time of day, trying to appeal to those who would be most likely to listen at a given time of day, tailored to the interests and quirks of local residents. Today with huge corporations owning hundreds and thousands of local radio stations this type of programming is a distant memory.

Early in the morning we had farm news because farmers in our region of the country were the first to rise and get to work. Livestock, corn, beans, wheat and sugar beet market prices were quoted and served with a big helping of country music. One of our hosts for that early morning broadcast was a country music singer who'd cut a few records (he carried a stack of blue-labeled 78s in the back of his beat up old car). I'd get up early, sign-on the radio station so I was required to wake him up and get him and his guitar on the air. He'd sing a song—introduce the pre-recorded market news—tell a story and sing another song—you get the idea.

While I was engineering records, playing commercials and operating his microphone button, I'd put together a fifteen minute local newscast and from 7 a.m. until 8 a.m. would read local news, weather and sports and then join the ABC and Intermountain Radio Networks during the time periods I wasn't stumbling through my own news. After 8 I would head for school and the programming would be turned over to another announcer to operate the control board.

About 9 a.m. an older gentleman who played a poorly tuned upright studio piano and sang songs would take the air from our studio adjacent to the control room. He was a career musician who knew a lot of songs. He would sing and play songs housewives might enjoy. There were many more stay-at-home mothers and wives in those days, enough that they represented a sizeable audience. A couple days a week a woman would join him to share recipes and parenting tips.

During the 50s in our town, we could only receive 2 or 3 television stations, located in Denver. They often didn't sign on the air until 2p.m. or 3p.m. in the afternoon. I remember running home from school to arrive in time to watch the latest episode of "Captain Video" on our new TV set. Those my age well remember the time spent staring at a "test pattern" waiting for the Star Spangled Banner kicking off another telecast session.

Back on the radio, mid-day we would again focus on news and market updates, then after lunch an afternoon of "grown-up" music that included 50s artists like, *Patti Page, Perry Como* and *Frankie Carle* (a favorite of the station manager's, I'd have to look for Frankie Carle albums when I journeyed to the warehouse in Denver). At 5 p.m. each weekday, I would be appointed the task of again operating the control board and reading the local news inserts because I was the only board operator who hadn't repeatedly mistimed the local commercial inserts during the Alex Dreier network news broadcast. It was a program the manager, listened to each evening on his way home from work and he would get very upset if it wasn't timed correctly.

Alex Dreier made his mark as a radio television newsman covering Berlin during the Second World War and at other times covering tense racial issues in Chicago, his home base. As the war escalated, Dreier chose to leave his then hometown, Honolulu one day before the Japanese bombed Pearl Harbor. In later years he enjoyed acting in films and television dramas. He passed away at the age of 86 in 2000. His daily radio broadcast became a national mainstay in the late 50s.

I would make a quick run to the candy store to get a bag of gum drops and flirt with the clerk, then on to the drive-in that sponsored my request program each night to get the information about specials I was to advertise on my broadcast that evening. I was usually treated to a burger and fries basket.

After the dinner break I would return with my high school requests, example: "From Paul to Mary, from Dick to Sally, To Pink Socks from JB—Here's Buddy Knox who is lookin' for a "Party Doll". A couple songs later each of the girls would respond, calling me and asking me to tell the boys they are not "party girls" or "that kind of girl". "From Mary to Hank, From Pink Socks to JB, from Sally to Dick Sorry guys not that kind of girl here's "*Just your* Dream" (I mean 'Just A Dream") with Jimmy Clanton."

My first and only year of College I was into folk music and for the final hour of our broadcast day (11 PM—Midnight) I started a new program called *After Hours* featuring the *Kingston Trio, Judy Collins, Oscar Brand*, the *Limelighters*, the *Brothers Four* and even an occasional live performance by *The Serendipity Singers* who were attending Colorado University in nearby Boulder at the time and had a huge hit record entitled "*Beans in my Ears*". I'd put a little "cool jazz" and old time blues into the mix. I'd try to talk more softly, thinking I could sound a little "cooler".(I'd actually turn down the lights in the control room and light a cigarette which is now a control room taboo because the smoke coats the electrical connections and ruins the equipment). In those days, unlike today, the announcer was given the freedom to choose songs, the order in which they were played and create a mood. It required creativity and you would work to sound professional but still sound as though you were in the room with the listener having a conversation.

During those evenings my high school friends would often show-up at the radio station to watch me work. My buddies took great delight when I would turn on the microphone, lower my voice as much as I could and speak loudly (trying to project). They would take turns amidst giggles to mock me as soon as the microphone was off. During network breaks, we'd grab old 78 records being tossed away and throw them like Frisbees at the radio tower behind the station, hoping to shatter them.

Through those early years I was gradually teaching myself to be a "news man". Because I read much of the news on the air, I was given the title of "News Director" my junior year in high school. I would listen closely to the broadcasts of Edward R. Murrow (who always smoked during his television broadcasts). I even started smoking, not to look cool but to develop that great gravelly masculine voice quality. A few years later, when I started working as a television news anchor I would consciously try to copy the delivery style of David Brinkley.

The station engineer installed police monitors and a two-way radio in my car so whenever I heard something happening, be it a car accident, a fire, a shooting or a fight I would jump in the car and rush to the scene to provide an on-scene first hand report.

When I was but a junior in High School (it was 1959), I joined a professional organization the *Radio Television News Directors Association.* The organization's national meeting that year was in San Francisco. I decided I would attend. I started smoking a pipe and wearing a man's hat in an effort to look older. My first test at the event came when we were all invited to see a new play "Under the Yum Yum Tree" headed for Broadway. During the play, alcoholic drinks were served and I was served without any questions. I felt I'd pulled it off. At our first banquet I sat beside the ABC Radio Network News Manager and managed to maintain a reasonable conversation with him about broadcast news. Either I was a good actor or he knew and was being polite but I was amazed at my ability to not act my true age and felt very "sophisticated" when I boarded the plane back to Denver.

There were a couple of live-on-scene reports I'd never forget. There had been a shooting at a seedy motel. A local police officer, Jim Longworth had repeatedly been called to a disturbance at the motel where a couple was loudly and continuously arguing with one another. Longworth had warned them to calm down or they would be arrested. After two warnings Longworth was again called. When Longworth entered the room the man reached into a desk drawer, pulled out a .22 caliber pistol and shot Longworth at close range in the neck. The man threw down the gun and started to run. His wife picked up the gun and shot her husband in the back as he fled.

When I arrived the man was lying dead in the parking lot, just a few feet from where I'd parked the car. The ambulance had just arrived and attendants were loading a gurney carrying Officer Longworth into the vehicle. I rushed to the hospital as well, for Longworth was a close family friend. He was a strong, active and very likeable man. He was a longtime friend of my mother. We'd actually travelled a couple of times with him to his home town to meet his parents who lived in a small town between Denver and Colorado Springs called Castle Rock. He would often stop by our house for a visit.

He spent the rest of his life paralyzed from the neck down. He fought a tough battle but died twelve years after the shooting in 1974. The mental picture of Jim being placed on an ambulance gurney and rushed into the emergency room has never left my head.

Another image or scene that has never left my mind occurred a few weeks earlier on December 14, 1961. I was in my first year of college and I was also working full-time at the radio station. I was preparing my early morning newscast when I heard the police monitor call for a highway patrol unit to respond to a train-vehicle accident at a country crossing a few miles outside of town.

The scene was littered with children's shoes, pieces of clothing, brightly wrapped Christmas presents, cards, bits of paper, notebooks. I looked past the wreckage to the empty snow covered fields beyond to see dozens of people running on foot through the fields toward the accident scene. Sherriff's deputies freed the bus driver, Duane Harms from the wreckage. Miraculously he wasn't badly injured. Because angry and frightened residents were physically rushing to the scene, Harms was quickly taken from the scene and held at an undisclosed location.

There were thirty-eight people aboard the large sixty-foot long bus. The bus was carrying children who were attending Delta School, a country school East of Greeley, Arlington Grade School in Greeley, Meeker Junior High School in Greeley and Greeley High School. They ranged in age from 6 to 16. Twenty children died, sixteen were injured. The dead were immediately taken to the old Greeley National Guard Amory and covered with white sheets. The injured were taken by ambulance and private cars to Weld County General Hospital where seventeen doctors were called into service.

The accident occurred at an open diagonal crossing located 2 miles east and 1 mile south of the Greeley suburb, Evans. Close to the accident site was a house. I walked to that house because as it happened my two-way car radio was malfunctioning. When I was admitted to the house I found children, many crying and injured lying on the floor. The woman who lived there was an aid at the Greeley hospital and the ambulances hadn't yet arrived. She told me to use her phone, she was too busy to use it. I called the radio station and was told ABC News in New York was patched in and was going to put me on the air live. The sound of crying children in the background brought the reality of the tragedy to those listening to that report. The rest of that day was a blur of feeding reports via phone to other networks, radio stations and even newspaper reporters from nearly everywhere, not just nationally but foreign media as well.

That afternoon inspectors from the Interstate Commerce Commission arrived in Greeley to begin an intensive investigation. A few weeks later I sat with the young driver, Duane Harms and his wife during a formal ICC hearing on the cause of the accident a few weeks later. Harms had worked as a custodian at the grade school and also drove the school bus each day. The train was a Union Pacific Streamliner called "The City of Denver". It was traveling at 73 miles per hour when the collision occurred. That morning the train was running 3 hours behind its regular schedule. The train was moved a few hundred feet down the tracks and held there for an hour after the accident. The passengers were not allowed off the train. The crew was later called back to Greeley from Denver for questioning.

An eyewitness at the scene said the school bus stopped, then rolled onto the tracks and was struck by the train from the rear. The train's crew contended the bus had not stopped. The entire mid-section of the bus was destroyed. That particular day it was so cold the windows in the crowded bus were frosted over and they wouldn't defrost. The children on the bus were excited about the special events at school for the holiday and were being unusually loud, so the driver didn't hear the warning horns.

One woman I later interviewed said she'd been called unexpectedly to work that day and had told her children she'd drop them off school on her way to work so they wouldn't have to wait for the bus in the cold. The temperature on that clear day was well below freezing. It was the only day her children did not board that bus.

More than forty years later the memory of that frightening day returned. The Rocky Mountain News in Denver featured a 31-part series of reports focusing on the long term effects that the accident had on the families of the victims and on the community itself. In the newspaper there were hundreds of comments tagged on those reports posted online by people who well remembered that day.

There was another unplanned, sad and strange occurrence that morning. When I finished that first report from the scene and signed off, the announcer on-duty simply grabbed a record to play, not looking at what song was scheduled next. Incredibly it was a Frankie Carle recording of *"The Acheson, Topeka and the Santa Fe"*.

Chapter Two

The Music,
Public Speaking
and Parents

S ince the age of 5 I've been fascinated by music. I found an old violin in my Grandfather's attic and was told if I learned to play it someday I would have the violin. In the first grade I gave my first public performance. My Grandmother was watching in the audience and on the way home she praised my performance and said the violin was mine. I played "Ole' Black Joe".

Through high school I entered a number of competitive music contests, played in the high school and college orchestras, the Junior Philharmonic orchestra, the Greeley Philharmonic and for two consecutive years the Colorado High School All-State Orchestra at the University of Colorado campus in Boulder.

I was fortunate to have absolutely top rate violin instructors, Henry T. Ginsburg and his wife Blanche. According to the University of Northern Colorado archives, Ginsburg was the concertmaster of the Denver Symphony for 20 years. He was born in New York. He was an incredibly accomplished violinist. He performed as a classical soloist traveling throughout the nation. When he was seventeen he traveled on the "Chautauqua Circuit" nationwide. He settled in Denver after five years on the road. In Denver he became Director of the Wolcott

Conservatory of Music, which later became the Denver College of Music. In the late 1920s Ginsburg organized the Denver String Quartet which became nationally known.

In the very early days of radio he became the music director for KOA radio where he would conduct an orchestra for a weekly nationwide radio broadcast called the *General Electric Hour*, and another broadcast called *McMurtry's Golden Memories*. For many years he conducted the America Theater Orchestra for which he actually orchestrated scores for the silent movies. He was the concert master for Denver's Elitch Gardens famous summer concerts, and in the early days of the Central City Operas he was the concert master of that orchestra.

In 1931 Henry Ginsburg moved to Greeley to teach at Colorado State Teachers College, later known as Colorado State College of Education and eventually the University of Northern Colorado. For twenty-seven years at the College he headed the Music Department, retiring in 1958. He and his wife were my instructors for more than ten years—first with Blanche, and then she asked him to work with me. Blanche was a gifted violinist and violist attending the college in the 1930s when Ginsburg arrived there to teach. They were married soon after.

When Dr. Ginsburg retired from teaching he opened a private studio with Blanche. It was located on the second floor of a clothing store in downtown Greeley. Ironically at the same time he opened his studio, I was helping move our radio station broadcast studios from the edge of town (in front of the broadcast tower) to a suite on the second floor of the same downtown building, in fact directly across the hall from the Ginsburg studio. It provided the opportunity for me to have a number of lengthy, very honest talks with him regarding my own future because I passed his studio door to access the radio studios.

He felt I had the talent to become a concert violinist (I didn't feel that confident) however he'd noticed the amount of time I spent at the radio station and repeatedly, in a fatherly kind of way, warned me of the excessive number of hours a concert violinist must keep practicing. He said a music career required an infinite commitment to practice. For me that was a needed reality check. Although I spent many hours trying to perfect my violin skills under the close scrutiny of my instructors, I actually considered practicing to be more therapeutic than compelling. I didn't fully understand then, but it dawned on me in later years that

I was very angry growing up and the faster and louder I played that violin, the better I would feel, often ending a practice session totally exhausted.

The Speech Meets

I was also very involved in high school debate and speech competitions. We frequently traveled in our instructor's car as a group, headed for these competitions. I didn't realize it at the time, but I was extremely fortunate to have a tough honest and caring speech teacher. I didn't realize until looking back a few years later, how much time and energy she gave to pack those of us involved in competitions into her personal older model Mercedes and drive all over three states to compete.

I remember one night, very late in the evening a couple of years after graduation, I was pulling a disc jockey shift in Casper, Wyoming. It was late in the evening and I received a phone call from one of her current students. A group of her students were with her headed for another speech competition and had been listening to my broadcast as they crossed Wyoming. The caller said she just wanted me to know they were checking up on my progress.

As it turned out her classes proved to be valuable to me because I would later do political analysis, commentaries and editorials and being taught in high school about debate, rhetorical questioning, logic development, impromptu speaking, original oratory and even dramatic reading was very helpful.

I was an only child. My mother was very social and very outgoing. My dad was the opposite, he didn't care much for socializing and didn't talk very much. She'd held a number of interesting jobs before she left my dad and me, including legal secretary, jail matron, and a Chamber of Commerce employee tasked with coordinating publicity and promotions for the annual local rodeo and celebration. It was a July 4th Celebration entitled "Go West With Greeley". In later years it was re-titled the "Greeley Stampede" and is today advertised as one of the largest PRCA sanctioned rodeos in the nation featuring entertainment and carnival attractions, much like a very large fair.

She'd made several appearances on Denver radio and television programs promoting the event including repeated appearances on former band leader Pete Smythe's very popular TV show. She also made annual appearances with two well-known radio farm broadcasters, Carl Herdsman and Evan Slack, who later in life I would meet. Evan actually remembered my mother when I met him many years later.

My Mother

Each year my mother worked for the Chamber, we had unusual guests stay at our house. Once, the entire French "Kayaking" team stayed with us for a week, none of whom spoke English. We frequently had cowboys competing in the rodeo staying at our home. My Dad was a pilot. He'd learned to fly and later taught military trainees to fly B-29 bombers when he joined the Army Air Corps the same year I was born, 1942. My grandfather died in the same hospital at which I was born in Garden City, Kansas several weeks after I was born. In fact my grandfather's last request before passing was to see the new baby.

My grandfather, Leroy Larry Cooper (My name is officially Larry Leroy) died of a ruptured appendix. My dad was stationed at Hays,

Kansas during the war and luckily was never sent on foreign missions. He and my mom were married in 1940. She was 18, he was 19. After the war he worked for my uncle (my Dad's brother-in-law) who was also a pilot, a somewhat infamous pilot. His name was Norm Kramer. Norm would gain his 15 minutes of fame when an engine on the Beech craft Bonanza he was flying caught fire and while the plane was still flying he actually crawled out onto the wing of the craft and extinguished the flames, then landed the plane safely (an especially difficult maneuver considering he was a physically large man). He also operated the airport for the city of Alamosa, Colorado. Norm was better known as the pilot for former Colorado Governor Dan Thornton. Governor Thornton was a much loved and very colorful individual.

He was born in Hall County, Texas, the son of a sharecropper. His family moved via covered wagons to Lubbock, Texas when he was a child. He went to high school in Lubbock and was very active in 4H. In fact he was named the Texas State 4H President. He attended, with the help of a football scholarship, UCLA in Los Angeles, graduating with honors. Young Thornton operated a filling station to help meet his expenses during college. It was at the service station he met Harry Warner of Warner Brothers Film Studio. Warner offered Thornton a three year contract to act in his movies. Thornton didn't like the Hollywood lifestyle and instead took a job working at an oil field derrick where he saved enough money to buy a dilapidated ranch in Arizona and a few head of cattle. That was in 1937. Three years later his cattle swept the awards at the Los Angeles Western Livestock Show and at Denver's National Western Livestock Show. The Thorntons then moved their ranching operations to a property near Gunnison, Colorado. His Herefords became a symbol of quality for livestock. In 1945 his Herefords were selling for as much as $50,000 a head. When he decided to sell his entire herd more than ten-thousand people showed up in Gunnison for his sale. His auction netted a record $860,264.

In 1948 Thornton was drafted to run on the Republican ballot for state senator. He ran unopposed. Former governor Ralph Carr died just twenty days before the 1950 gubernatorial election. The party drafted Thornton to run for governor even though there wasn't much time to campaign. With my Uncle Norm as his pilot, Thornton flew to every town in Colorado, averaging eleven speeches each day. It worked for Thornton, he won the election by 23,000 votes. Norm's brother Mark was Thornton's business manager and became his right hand man when Thornton was elected governor. I remember as a child being picked up by my aunt Edna, who was at that time married to Norm Kramer, for a driving trip with her and my Grandmother. Edna was driving Governor Thornton's Lincoln. It was very much into character for my Aunt. Edna had flaming red hair, smoked with a bejeweled cigarette holder, and she had this deep dramatic "actress kind of voice".

In 1968, when as a Denver news reporter I flew along with the Colorado Delegates to the National Republican Convention in Miami, I sat beside former Governor Thornton during the flight. Even with the family connections and my trip in his car it was the first time I'd ever met him. He was unassuming, with a great sense of humor and I thoroughly enjoyed the time we talked together. During his last election campaign his opponent characterized him as a rich Texan. Thornton countered that he and his wife arrived in Colorado heavily in debt and Colorado had been good enough to them to allow them to clear their debt but they were certainly not wealthy. Thornton served two terms as Colorado's Governor from 1951 to 1956. He was one of a short list of 5 that Dwight Eisenhower was considering for his running mate. Richard Nixon was selected. I personally think Thornton would have been preferable.

My Dad had earlier worked for Norm Kramer flying mail over the Colorado Rockies. He later worked as a flight instructor in Greeley and an agricultural chemical spray pilot. In later years he worked, as did his Dad before him at a lumber yard. When I was a child my Dad and I often flew in small planes to visit his friends, usually landing in farm fields near a farmhouse or to visit my Grandmother's home in Garden City, Kansas. He would frequently rent an aircraft and fly to New Mexico or Arizona to pick up cowboys headed for the rodeo.

I still remember my Dad and I flying to Kansas where record snowfalls had stranded thousands of livestock. It was 1948, I was 6 years old. I was left in the country with my uncle while my Dad flew emergency drop missions to feed the livestock. The snow was so high my uncle cleared a tunnel to pass through the front door and you could walk up to the roof and slide down on a sled. I thought it was great fun. I don't believe my Uncle agreed.

When I was thirteen I worked part-time as an usher at a local movie theater. One day the manager approached me and told me my mother was in the lobby and needed to talk to me. She told me we had to go to the airport fast because my father's plane may have crashed. Outside the theater there was a Colorado Highway Patrol car waiting to take us to the airport. At the airport we were told there was a plane down and the pilot's name was Robert Cooper (my dad's name). As we were fighting back the tears another plane landed in front of us. It was my dad with his cowboy passengers, completely unaware of what was causing all the excitement. The plane that crashed was piloted by "Robert Cooper" (same name) and the numbers on the plane's wing closely matched those on my dad's rented plane but thankfully for us (unfortunately for him) it was a different "Robert Cooper". My mother urged my dad to find another line of work. They frequently argued about that.

My dad (who always denied my repeated attempt to get him to teach me how to fly) eventually gave up flying after his best friend also a pilot from his home town was killed when his plane crashed. My Dad searched for and found the plane wreckage. I still own the propeller from that crashed aircraft. I find irony, thinking back, in the fact my dad quit flying because of the risk of accidents, yet met his death at the young age of 56 when he fell down the back stairs at home.

The same year there was a new attraction at our local rodeo and carnival. It was called "*The Dancing Waters*". It was housed in a large circus-type tent with a lot of water pipes covering about half the tent. It was devised by a German Engineer. I've done a little research on its history which dates way back to 1928 when a German Engineer first created the show. His name was Otto Przystawik. In 1951 his show was featured at the Berlin Industrial Exhibit. The creator's son, Gunter travelled with the show throughout Europe and the United States and trained staff for proper set-up and operation. I've learned my mother was one of only nine people in the world who was trained to operate the key console, a device that is "played" much like a pipe organ.

The water movements lagged behind the signals being sent by the operator just a few seconds so the trick was to align the movements with proper application of the keys (the keys had to be pushed a few seconds ahead of the music to remain on beat) and coordinate that with the movement of a grid of moving colored flood lights. My mother was an accomplished pianist and organist and soon learned to operate the contraption.

It is estimated the display was seen by more than a million people at New York's Radio City Music Hall. An article in the Los Angeles Times about the Dancing Waters claimed the full show used several thousand feet of steel pipe, 19 electric motors, 4,000 jets, 68,000 watts of power and 38 tons of water. Obviously the Carnival touring version wasn't that elaborate. The attraction toured throughout the United States, featured at many of the larger fairs especially in California, my mother becoming a part of that show.

I remember my father and I driving to Denver (about 50 miles away) one night (we hadn't seen my mother for weeks) to attend the premier of the 1955 film "Anastasia" which starred *Ingrid Bergman* and *Yul Brynner* at the *Denver Theater*. Actually we were going there to meet my mother whom we rarely saw anymore. Apparently, unbeknownst to me they had already discussed divorce. There was a special intermission with entertainment provided by *The Dancing Waters*, which is why my mother was in Denver but didn't plan to stop at home in Greeley.

In 1970 *The Dancing Waters* were installed at the Disneyland Hotel in Anaheim and in 1992 it was updated and revised to include fiber optic displays and more modern lighting technology and its name was changed to *The Fantasy Waters Show*. That too has since ended but certainly the original Dancing Waters was a forerunner to the spectacular show featured in front of the Las Vegas Bellagio Hotel.

My mother toured with the Dancing Waters show to California where she was offered a new job, helping to promote and organize the annual Indio, *California Date Festival*. My mother sent me photos of her in a harem costume, in a cow girl outfit, and riding a camel and an elephant in her harem costume.

This particular event featured more exotic animals than traditional livestock. It attracted some elite backers with an annual pageant choreographed by a Broadway Director. Indio was very close to Palm Springs and Palm Desert. That drew attention from some of the area's wealthier more famous residents. The fair also attracted thousands of Canadian "snowbirds" who annually spend their winters there, returning to Canada when the weather warmed north of the border.

Many years later, while working for the state of California and setting up informational displays at the more than one hundred plus fairs in the state, I visited the lobby of the Date Festival offices and studied a number of historic photos on the walls of attractive young ladies wearing harem costumes while mounted on camels and elephants. I didn't see any of my mother's photos there but it certainly brought memories.

About this time it became apparent to me my mother was not planning to return home. One day as my Dad and I were beginning a road trip to Kansas he handed me a letter to read he'd received from my mother. She informed him that she had filed for a "quickie" divorce in Mexico and they were no longer married.

While working in Indio my mother met a man who at the time managed an Indio mortuary. They were married in April, 1955 at a restaurant and bar, *The Idle Spurs Steak House* located on a bluff overlooking the city of Barstow, California, where his parents lived. Shortly before that marriage ceremony occurred, my father received another letter and a packet of documents. My mother wanted him to re-sign the documents because she had learned the Mexican divorce was not legally recognized in California.

Visiting Relatives

Being raised as an only child by a single father I was frequently sent to relative's homes for spring breaks, holiday periods and sometimes parts of summers. My grandmother, Mildred Cooper, had moved from her home in Garden City, Kansas purchasing an old mansion she converted to a bed and breakfast located adjacent to the *Garden of the Gods* in Manitou Springs, a suburb of Colorado Springs, Colorado. Red Crags Lodge was a gorgeous three story Victorian structure over a century old with several fireplace equipped rooms on the second floor and a third floor apartment unit Grandmother rented out. We labeled each room by design color, the "Blue Room", the "White Room," "Red Room" etc. The house sat on three acres complete with an original carriage house, a perfectly manicured lawn and a walking trail to the top of the hill where there was a barbeque pit and a 360 view of the mountains, including 14,000 foot Pikes Peak and the Garden of the Gods. The house was built with 3 to 4 foot thick red rocks at the foundation. There was a formal living room with a full sized Grand Piano and an organ adjacent to what my Grandmother called *the Sun Room* now referred to as *The Solarium*.

Red Crags Lodge

I would spend many non-school periods "helping" Grandmother. Grandmother would frequently tell vacationers staying at the Lodge that I made a pretty good maid, until I complained one morning (while cleaning the room reserved for newly married couples) that a newly married couple was so careless they'd left toe-nail clippings all over the floor. In fact the mysterious clippings were rice.

I would frequently get to go with patrons of the Lodge to guide them (or they let me think I was guiding them) to the many tourist attractions. including *the Seven Falls, the Cave of the Winds, Cheyenne Mountain* (beneath which NORAD Tracks all things in Space), the famed *Cheyenne Mountain Zoo* and of course the famous *Broadmoor Hotel* where world class ice skaters and Olympians train. My grandmother treated me several times to a movie at the Broadmoor. There was a theater in the hotel that featured classic films. I remember watching the original version of the film that was eventually made into a Broadway musical and a movie called *My Fair Lady*. The version I saw with my

Grandmother was the 1938 British film entitled *"Pygmalion"* starring *Leslie Howard* and *Wendy Hiller*. I also spent many hours at Red Crags listening to and loving my Grandmother's unusual record collection which included original recordings of *Enrico Caruso* and *John Phillip Souza* Marches, I don't know why but I was fascinated with both.

During one of my visits to Red Crags I got what I thought was a great idea. I set up a card table, covered it with a table cloth and made a little sign that said "Tourist Information". I stacked brochures my grandmother displayed in the hallway of Red Crags and put a little jar on the table labeled "tips" setting this all up on the roadway at the bottom of the hill on which Red Crags was located. Several cars actually stopped, people would look through my brochures and ask me questions and left change in my jar. I was getting excited; until a police car pulled up. The officer asked me what I was doing, and then asked me for my city business license. I said I didn't know I had to have one. The officer helped me take my display down and carry it back up to the house, then told my grandmother I could get in trouble if I continued to offer my services. He told her someone in the neighborhood had actually called the police about my questionable business venture.

My dad later married a woman about fifteen years his senior. Their wedding took place in the Sun Room at Red Crags and I was the Best Man. She was a widow with two very attractive teenage daughters. I was quickly moved from my main floor bedroom to take permanent residency in the basement. My step mother also filled most of the basement with antique furniture she had saved or collected from relatives, ending a series of regular parties I hosted with my friends in our basement. My step-mother (Marjorie Kingsley Cooper) was fun to talk with although I never really got to know her. She did through the years consistently call and send cards, even after my Dad died of injuries suffered when he fell down the back stairs of their home in Greeley.

My wife and I at that time were living in Scottsbluff, Nebraska. He had been taken to a hospital in Fort Collins and when we arrived there he was on life support. I was given instructions by my step mother to make a decision when to take him off the machine. After more than a week with no sign of brain activity I made that decision. It was not an easy decision. My Dad was only 56 at the time. He and Marge both loved to play golf and their years together were peaceful. A few years after his death, she remarried again. She passed away at the age of 90 a few years ago at a nursing home.

I spent several vacations with my mother's sister Ardith and her husband, John Burton. John was identified in a magazine story as "America's last real cowboy". John was raised on a Nebraska Ranch. He received national recognition when he rode his horse "Dixie" from Nebraska to Arizona and through the Grand Canyon, then onto California then back to Nebraska.

When my aunt Ardith and John met and started dating, she was working as a nurse at Denver's Children's Hospital. The first time I met John, my dad and I had driven to Denver to visit Ardith in her downtown area apartment. When we arrived there was a horse tied up in the street behind a truck pulling a horse trailer. It was a rare sight in the urban area. John had stopped by to see her before heading back to the mountains to work.

John had a very practical way of looking at life. He worked very hard and had a unique yet simple and straight-forward philosophy work hard, rest and play (meaning ride a rubber inner tube on the nearby river) then work hard again. He talked slowly but to the point, not wasting a lot of words. He would relax in the evening listening to *Burl Ives* or the *Sons of the Pioneers* on old 78 records. The first time I stayed with John and Ardith it was during a spring break. I was about 11 years old. My dad drove me up to the Colorado high mountain country where I was to join them for two weeks during spring break from school. John was leading a cowboy crew in the mountains above Kremmling, Colorado on a ranch owned by then State Legislator Fay DeBerard. DeBerard served in the Colorado Legislature for 23 years and for many years was on the Board of Directors for Denver's National Western Livestock Show. DeBerard raised several national champion Hereford and breeding animals.

Ardith and John were living in a tiny trailer with one double bed, one single bed and a very small kitchen. There was an outhouse and one of my morning chores was to walk, carrying a large bucket about three-quarters of a mile to a spring to get water. John reserved the oldest, calmest, smallest sized horse he could find for me, gave me some quick lessons on riding the animal, and a quick review on how to help the crew herd livestock up the mountains to higher ground which was our job for the week. Each morning Ardith would arise before dark and begin preparing an unbelievable breakfast for a total of eight people. John would immediately go outside to the corral and try to mount a gorgeous Palomino Stallion who did not want to be mounted. It would buck and kick and jerk around in circles and finally give-up. Then John would help me get on my horse and each morning he would remind me that his stallion was not people-friendly and had once kicked one rider to death. John would say "Just don't walk behind that horse—ever".

To my surprise I was a pretty good cattle chaser. When one of the animals would start to stray, left or right of the herd I was to spot them, trot over and get them back in line. It was fun and I was getting pretty confident. Then, at midweek we stopped for lunch alongside a mountain creek with cold clear water you could drink without treating the water in any way. I bent down, took a drink then as I returned to my lunch made a critical error. I was thinking about how cold and pure that mountain stream water tasted, not about where I was walking. I walked directly behind that stallion. In a flash I was on the ground mumbling to myself. John rushed to my side saying "My God that horse got him right at the edge of his temple". One of the crew rode his horse at a gallop back to the camp trailer to get a pick-up truck. By the time we returned to the trailer I had fully recovered. I sheepishly told John I was sorry I forgot. He simply said "you'll know better next time."

In later years John and Ardith purchased a lot of grazing land (25,000 Acres) located in the Nebraska Sand Hills, adjacent to the South Dakota border. In South Dakota John found the remnants of an old log house that he purchased for little money. He and Ardith got a flat bed truck and managed with some help from friends to lift that old house onto the truck bed and very slowly moved it about 45 miles to the very remote site he had selected in Nebraska, 15 miles from the nearest road. He dug out a foundation for the house and in the process uncovered multiple rattlesnake pits. When a rattlesnake would start buzzing John would remove his belt, take aim at the snake's head and flick it hard with his belt buckle. He said he'd killed more rattlers than he could count, just using his belt buckle. John eventually sculpted that old house into a solid and well constructed four bedroom log home with a full basement and a very large kitchen for Ardith.

During subsequent years I would visit John and Ardith with some frequency, usually when it was time to mow and rake his alfalfa fields. My job was to rake with a rig attached to an old Model A car. He'd cut the top off and made it into a tractor. John still did much of his field work using a pair of beautiful work horses he maintained for years. He did purchase a small tractor one year but it didn't match up for John, he said "the horses don't keep breaking down". I had great respect for John. He and Ardith were the hardest working couple I've ever known but they shared an inner peace that was indefinable.

John and Ardith had two children, a girl with beautiful red hair named Velvet and a boy named Mitch. My wife and I and our children attended Velvet's wedding held at the VFW hall in the tiny town of Valentine, Nebraska. It was a story-book wedding with the bride arriving in John's best horse-drawn wagon and all-night dancing at the Valentine VFW Hall. She married a tall dark and very handsome young ranch boy who later became a mail man in Wyoming. After a stint with the U.S. Air Force Velvet's brother Mitch, who learned to ride a horse before he could walk, moved to Southern California to work on a ranch located on one of the Channel Islands, off the coast from Ventura. Mitch got married, had his own family and has since worked as an electrician. A few years ago, when Ardith visited her doctor's office for a routine check-up she suffered a fatal heart attack during a stress test. John later retired to a small property in Arizona.

Thinking about Velvet's wedding makes me think about another unusual wedding for which I played the music. It occurred on a ranch located in the mountains above Chico, California. The ranch was owned by an executive for *Sunset Magazine* whose daughter was getting married. He'd built a dance floor in the woods and set-up lighting using portable power generators. The guests were picked up at the main ranch house and transported on four wheel drives to a beautiful meadow adjacent to a river canyon. Pat and I were taken to the spot earlier to set-up and test our music system and lighting.

When I tested everything to see if it worked and sounded good, an entire herd of cattle strolled into the meadow. They were the first guests to arrive. It was as though they were curious what that strange music was about. When the other guests arrived and were all seated, right at sundown, the bride and her father rode over the crest of a hill in a horse drawn wagon. It would have made a great cover for Sunset Magazine. The bride's name was Jeannie and as soon as I saw the wagon at the top of the hill I was to play *Jeannie with the light brown hair*. It was almost breathtaking with the song ending just a the bride stepped down from the wagon to begin her wedding march. The partying didn't end until sunrise. Another life lesson, often self-created opportunities result in great mind's eye memories.

Yes Dorothy, it is definitely Kansas

As I was growing up I was also sent, for periods of a week to a month, to another Aunt and Uncle's home. My uncle Leo Meeker and his three brothers were all wheat farmers as was their father. Leo's wife Jean was one of my Dad's four sisters. Leo owned a wheat farm located about a mile outside of Dighton, Kansas and a second located near Scott City, Kansas.

My memories of those visits are scattered and bring to mind these scenes:

- Frogs by the thousands hopping all over a rain soaked dirt road
- Wheat combine crews waking one another up in the bunk house by setting off cherry bombs beneath their beds
- Drinking what had to be the best sweet-tea in the country while eating sandwiches sitting in a wheat field in the shade of a combine
- Being fascinated with a large metal tank in my Uncle's farmyard where thousands of minnows and small fish were being prepared for their role as fishing bait.
- My uncle stomping over the mud covered driveway to an outbuilding to fire up a noisy but productive generator so we might have lights during frequent storms.
- My older cousin Kent and I being left alone on the Scott City farm with a freezer full of steaks, some canned veggies and a World War Two Jeep truck rigged with floodlights. We were there to jump on the truck with shovels and every two or three hours all night long, drive out to the fields with shovels to plug water flows and channel the flow to another row or stream
- Riding with my aunt 60 miles to Garden City (the City of my birth) just so she could treat me to a fresh ice cream cone

- Climbing with my Uncle to the top of a newly constructed, very high concrete wheat elevator. You could see for miles from the top.
- Visiting the Shasta Soda canning plant in Garden City after my Uncle invested in the facility. He was convinced it was the best soda in the World
- My uncle taking great delight in watching me in his mirror in the back seat of his big ole Chrysler, while I was starting to take a swallow of an ice cold bottle of soda, and just as I put the bottle to my lips, gunning the car so it would splatter all over me. He was somewhat grumpy and gruff but that would crack him up every time.
- It seemed to me he bought a new Chrysler every year and would frequently hit 100 miles per hour when driving the one mile into town.
- I remember standing on a small pile of dirt looking out over miles of flat wheat land watching a brown dust storm headed our way. This is very reminiscent of the great dust storms of the 1930s which resulted in the formation of the Federal Agency that was my last employer before retirement, the old Soil Conservation Service, renamed in the 90s the Natural Resources Conservation Service—an agency that helps farmers conserve the land.

It was without a doubt Kansas.

The new Step Dad

I met my step-father Floyd O'Donnell when I turned fifteen. His friends called him "Digger O'Dell" because he was a mortician with an Irish heritage. When I arrived in Los Angeles and got off the airplane I was greeted by my mother, who somewhat awkwardly and nervously offered me a cigarette (which I declined, although I had secretly smoked I couldn't do it in front of her). When we arrived at the car it was a very large and long Cadillac. I'd never taken a ride in a Cadillac before. It was used as a funeral family car. Every time we stopped the car at a stop sign or turned a corner I would slide off the back seat onto the floor.

The seat was probably 5 to 6 feet behind the front seat so there was nothing to lean against or hold onto to keep you from sliding and the seat cover was plastic and very slick. At this time in history seat belts were not built in to cars. My new step father found the situation to be quite amusing. We stopped at a Hilton Hotel restaurant to eat. I'd never been in a hotel that elaborate and was shocked beyond belief when I looked at the menu and saw a hamburger was $5.00. Back home I could buy a hamburger steak, fries and a soda for $1.25.

Years later, when Pat and I were married, we again flew to Los Angeles and my mother and step-father greeted us, again driving the mortuary's family car. This time Pat, who is all of 4"11" slid onto the floor with every movement. Again Floyd was delighted.

Life in a Mortuary—an Oxymoron

I would pay many visits to my mother and step-father through the years. They lived at funeral homes in Victorville and in later years at Thousand Oaks and at Oxnard. One night in Oxnard, a somewhat inebriated woman managed to drive her car through the front door of the funeral parlor, breaking a lot of glass and skewing the casket displays. She was not injured nor were any of the deceased residents, who I doubt really cared.

Spending vacation time in a mortuary is a bit bizarre. My stepfather's brother owned the Victorville funeral home located in the "High Desert" of California. Floyd was the Manager. Apple Valley was just over the hill. Apple Valley was the home of Roy Rogers and Dale Evans (and the stuffed horse Trigger who was on display then at the Roy Rogers Museum) The stuffed Trigger was recently sold at auction for $266,500.

The year I was seventeen I spent a month in Victorville helping my step-father with his ambulance service. At the time he operated the only ambulance in the High Desert. I went along to help lift patients (and in a few cases bodies) and drive when my stepfather tired. If the bed in the ambulance was unoccupied he would stretch out on the gurney and go to sleep while I drove. I remember the eerie feeling, while in the wee small hours of the morning, driving with the red lights of the ambulance flashing. The colored lights reflected on everything we passed, in otherwise complete darkness. The flashing lights and the dead quiet (we didn't turn on the siren for there was no traffic) created a mind's eye scene that was dramatic, even a bit bizarre. It was at times a somewhat gruesome endeavor.

We picked up the remains of a jet pilot who was ejected in flight when there was an engine failure. Although he had a parachute strapped to his back it did not release and he landed feet-first in the desert. The landing was so hard his hips were jammed up to his neck. We picked up a young mother and her 5 year old daughter. Her sports car convertible struck a large dip in the highway coming down from the San Bernardino Mountains and flipped end over end repeatedly. Both were in serious condition and the nearest hospital was 40 miles. I never really learned if they'd survived. We picked up the remains of a woman who lived alone on a remote desert ranch. She was over 100 years old and had fallen off her horse which she rode daily for many years until that fateful day. She was said to be a famous but extremely reclusive silent film star. That was the legend passed around by desert locals who I learned were basically very reclusive themselves and preferred as little contact with the outside world as possible. They were generally referred to as "those desert rats" by residents of area communities.

I made an effort, while spending that summer in the desert to get a radio shift at a radio station located inside the Apple Valley Inn, which was a fairly plush motel, bar and restaurant. The control room announcer looked directly through a large plate glass window at the swimming pool. As a teenage boy, that seemed to me to be a dream job. Announcing, spinning tunes and watching the young ladies lounge in bikinis. It would certainly beat the ambulance gig. Alas, I didn't get that job and ended up instead playing violin solos for funeral services at my step-father's mortuary chapel. My proudest accomplishment that summer was installing a speaker system throughout the funeral home to pipe in "appropriate music."

One weekend night we attended a *"Luau Night at the Apple Valley Inn."* I did meet a teenage girl there and we did dance, but the entire evening she said absolutely nothing, we just nodded at one another. Needless to say she was extremely shy as was I. We were told the band that night featured the same trumpet player heard on the *Perez Prado* recording of *"Cherry Pink and Apple Blossom White"* which was at the top of the charts at the time. Someone told me that night the trumpet solo for that recording was played by *Al Hirt*. I later learned it was actually *Maynard Ferguson*, a longtime lead for *Stan Kenton*. Ferguson lived at nearby Ojai and often sat in with Prado's group. I could hear him play that night long ago at the Inn but couldn't see over the crowd to identify him. I did remember thinking it didn't sound like Al Hirt. Years later when I had two boys of my own, I took each of them to Maynard Ferguson concerts with his own band and they each still talk of the experience. I was sad when Maynard passed away. He was a legendary player and a great showman.

When I graduated from high school I was awarded a fully paid music scholarship to Colorado State College of Education. I was getting a free ride to play violin. But I stubbornly kept my job at the radio station (by now fulltime), and signed up for a full class load including required courses in Algebra, Humanities, Advanced English, Earth Sciences and of course orchestra and music composition, public speaking, rhetorical debate and a then mandatory Reserve Officer Training Corps military class. I was also required to take a physical education class. Not being very physical I evaded the P.E. requirement by signing up for Square Dancing classes.

The partner I selected for Square Dancing classes (held at a very early 8 a.m.) was an extremely cute girl. Throughout the quarter we danced together. I really didn't think she would go out with me but toward the end of the quarter I got my nerve up and asked her out. She quickly said "yes". She said she wondered when I would ask. I wanted to make it a special night out so with another couple we drove to Denver to go to one of the city's famously classy and historic theaters to see the film "*Spartacus*." It was getting late as we headed home and we decided to stop at an all-night truck stop to get something to eat. I sat across the table from her. Suddenly a man, about 40 years old, wearing a dirty t-shirt with a pack of cigarettes rolled up in the sleeve pushed into the seat beside her. He had a big grin on his face and he started asking if we were on a date. He and I conversed for several minutes. He pushed closer to her and placed his hand over her hand on the table. I assumed he was someone she knew, although she quickly pulled her hand away. I don't recall what I said to him but I attempted to keep it friendly (thinking it was someone she knew). He finally left the table. When we returned to the car I asked her politely "By the way was that gentleman a relative of yours?" She looked at me angrily and said "I've never seen him before in my life! I was hoping you would suggest we all leave. You could have done something! He scared me to death!" She would never go out with me again.

Music wasn't my major course path, that was speech arts. However when I told the person who headed the speech department I wanted to become a broadcast journalist, he laughed and said I was "barking up the wrong school." This was pre-Watergate, before there was a rush to become "investigative reporters." Although as a freshman I did win the school's original oratory competition and represented the college at a regional college level competition (during which I, embarrassing as it was, forgot part of my mandatorily memorized speech). My presentation clearly reflected a timely debate at the time regarding the "domino theory" a frequently used excuse for our Vietnam involvement. The response to my inquiry about broadcast journalism prompted me to leave college and as it turned out to leave a potential career in music. In fact I never again picked up the violin.

Chapter Three

Leaving Home, Romancing and Moving On

One day I received a phone call from a woman in Boulder, Colorado. She and her husband owned a little radio station in Casper, Wyoming. She called me because she had seen an Associated Press story that I had contributed the most stories to the wire service in Colorado. She convinced me I was being presented a golden opportunity to become a real broadcast journalist.

I drove up to Casper one weekend to meet the station's manager. I was wined and dined at a colorful old restaurant that sat on the river. He assured me this would be a mutually beneficial transition. Many years later when the radio station at which I was working in California was being put on the auction block, I applied for a sales job at a small station located in (of all places) Victorville. I received an interesting response to my application. I mention this as another mind's eye memory. Life experience is mysteriously cluttered with odd coincidences. The manager and owner of the Victorville radio station wrote me a letter saying the job was mine if I really wanted it however he was personally insulted that the resume I provided failed to even mention the three months I had worked at the station he managed at the time in Casper.

On a very snowy and windy evening, early in 1962 I packed nearly everything I owned in the back of an old car and began the drive north, through historic Cheyenne, Wyoming then for more than 180 miles of windy snow-swept roadways. I could barely see through the blowing snow and the darkness. It was night and I'd begun to wonder if I'd somehow gotten completely lost. Finally I saw a dim neon sign reading "Motel". I stopped, entered the office and met one of the nicest women I've ever known. She displayed a warm friendly smile and obviously at a younger time in her life had been a beauty. She was a pianist-singer when she wasn't operating the motel. She shared ownership of this somewhat run-down motel with her boyfriend who was also a musician whose day job was selling insurance. Betty never married him but the couple remained together many years. She'd previously had a bad marriage and was intent on never again making a commitment like that.

That first night I told her I was hoping I'd found or was near the city of Casper, although the only lights I'd seen through the hundreds of miles of blowing snow were those at her motel. She assured me I'd found the right city. She actually poured me a strong drink and we chatted for about an hour. I don't believe any of her rooms were actually rented that night. She also owned the apartment building where she lived and happened to have an apartment available if I was interested. She said I looked honest and had a job promise and that was good enough for her. No deposit, in fact I wasn't required to pay anything until I'd worked long enough at the radio station to pay the rent. We became good friends through the 5 years I remained in Casper. I was barely eighteen at the time of my arrival but told anyone who asked I was twenty-one. She loved to talk politics and in fact secretly hosted clandestine meetings of the *John Birch Society* at her motel.

When I reported to work I was informed that in addition to serving as the News Director I would also be required to host a four hour rock and roll radio show daily. One Saturday I was on the air "Rockin' into the 60s from the Queen City of the Plains!" (Casper—Really?) when a dust covered old blue Chrysler pulled up in the station's drive-way. Four guys came to the door. I asked them through a door speaker who they were looking for. They were looking for me. They told me they were "*The Ventures.*"

The radio station was hosting a teen dance that night featuring the group whose record "*Walk Don't Run*" was holding onto the Billboard

Number One slot. I let them in and told them I would really like to interview them. I quickly pulled chairs into the small control room and plugged in a couple of extra microphones. I asked each to first give us their real name. When I got to the third band member he replied "I'm one of the Ventures" I said OK do you want to share your real name with us? He replied "I'm sorry I just can't think of it right now." One of his band members spoke up in his defense explaining the group had been stuck in that old Chrysler on the road for 36 straight hours trying to find Casper and they were extremely tired. Nonetheless the dance was a sell-out and the Ventures never missed a beat or a note.

About two weeks after that, we attempted to sponsor another dance. This one featured the *Ralph Marterie* Big Band, an event I volunteered to emcee. I loved big bands. At our high school back in Greeley the *Stan Kenton* Band had returned three years in a row for one week each, giving performances and actually working with our orchestra and our band. Stan Kenton, a piano player had a reputation for featuring experimental jazz in concert form and actually provided a training program for young college and high school musicians across the country.

Years later, while working for the State of California as an information officer I would learn that many of the original Kenton band members had retired to Sacramento and were teachers, worked at banks, a variety of jobs, one of them was actually the band teacher at a Sacramento High School. Occasionally they would get together and "jam," I caught one of those nights when Maynard Ferguson was in town to join them, they still sounded incredible. I realized many of these "celebrity" talents also depended on regular day jobs. They were "real people."

Back to Ralph Marterie, the turnout for our dance wasn't very good and Marterie and I spent some time just chatting with one another, mostly about what appeared to be at that time "the death of the big bands." He feared and rightly so they were being pushed off the map by the rush to rock and roll and the changing marketing climate in terms of promoting and selling records. Marterie even modernized some of his band's songs, working in an amplified guitar with a rock and roll beat. I find some irony in the fact that Marterie was one of the last one-night-stand big bands on the road continuing the practice until the mid-70s. Ralph Marterie passed away in 1978. Today there are a few veteran musicians and a number of younger gifted players who do tours playing original arrangements.

I saw the great trombonist *Buddy Morrow* and a big band touring under the name *"The Tommy Dorsey Band"* and I more recently enjoyed a group touring as *"The Glenn Miller Band."* I don't believe (or like to think that) the big bands will ever completely fade away. Unfortunately many of today's younger generations have never been exposed to the exciting sound of a big band (other than college marching bands). The audiences for the touring groups today are usually those of us old enough to remember 78 records. The Glenn Miller Band played a one-time appearance at a renovated theater here in Bozeman, Montana. I asked my 26 year old driver and friend Elizabeth if she would like to attend the concert with me. Her first response was "Who's Glenn Miller?" Because I suffer from Muscular Dystrophy I must remain on my mobility scooter so at the concert she and I were seated in the front row, directly in front of the band. Elizabeth, the daughter of a co-worker is an incredibly confident and beautiful young lady. After the concert (which she said she enjoyed tremendously) as the band members were dismantling music stands and putting instruments away, she and I started crossing in front of the stage to reach the aisle. She noticed one of the band members watching us, gave him her glowing smile and told him the concert was "great" to which he replied "Thank you so much for sitting in the front row" (implying it was rare to see great "eye-candy" in the front row of one of their performances). Most of the audience members that night were over 60.

That also reminds me, I was talking with Elizabeth as she drove me to work one day and I mentioned I'd been a big fan of the *Kingston Trio* back in the day, to which she replied she'd never heard of them. I told her **they** were the only singing group in history (including *the Beatles*) simultaneously having five albums on the list of the top ten selling albums in the World.

I last saw the Kingston Trio at a performance at Lake Tahoe a few years ago. The three old men limped up to the front of the stage, Dave Guard held his hands over his eyes to block out the bright stage lights and looked over the audience and said "My God—you all got so old!" Another unwelcome reminder of my increasing age, I remember the first live performance I attended of the Kingston Trio. They were opening for the *Benny Goodman Sextet* with the great jazz pianist *Teddy Wilson*. "I know Elizabeth—Who's Benny Goodman?"

I was fortunate as a teenager to have seen live performances by *Nat King Cole, Nelson Riddle, Patti Page, Harry James,* and others of the era. My year in college I helped set up the stage for the great orchestra leader *Montovani.* At that concert, after his orchestra's first song, he stopped the concert, asking the staff to remove a part of the curtain hanging over the front of the stage. He told me afterward "People who paid to see my orchestra want the full experience with the sound unhampered by decoration!" That same year, after recording an interview with the then popular *Bud and Travis,* folk singers I was given permission to record the entire concert for play-back on my "After Hours" broadcast. Today that would be unheard of without a lot of legal paperwork and analysis. Then I simply asked the performers if they would allow me to record the concert and use segments on my radio show and they said "Sure, no problem."

The World's Greatest Trumpet Player

A couple of years before my Wyoming adventure I'd talked about the same situation (the demise of the big bands) with another incredible musician who enjoyed spending time with music departments at high schools as he travelled across the nation. His name was *Rafael Mendez.* He too would stop at smaller cities to work with high school bands and orchestras.

He was often referred to as the "Heifetz of the Trumpet." He was considered by many musicians to be the "greatest trumpet player in the World" and I believe he really was. He made many recordings for Decca records, classical and big band. I made an appointment to visit him at the motel where he was staying one night and record a radio interview with him. His personal story was fascinating. He was literally born into a well known family orchestra in Mexico that frequently toured throughout the country. When he was just 4 years old his father started to teach him to play trumpet and a guitar. When he was 8 years old his entire family was captured by the revolutionary army headed by *Poncho Villa* and taken to their secret headquarters to entertain his army. After a few weeks Villa released the family but ordered young Rafael to remain. Villa was fascinated by the talent and skill displayed with the guitar and trumpet by this little boy. He told the boy he wanted him to be the bugle boy for his troops. He was eventually released and sent back to his family. He continued to play trumpet for the family's gigs and also played with a number of circus bands. When he was only 15 he joined the Mexican Army Band. He eventually moved to the United States working at a General Motors factory in Michigan. While working there he auditioned to join a professional band in Detroit and that led to a record contract with Decca Records.

Mendez raised twin sons, both of whom were accomplished trumpet players and even recorded an album with their father. Both became respected medical doctors. I have never heard any other trumpet player as expert at the craft. He spent two days at Greeley High School working with our orchestra and band, ending with a free concert for the community.

Back to Casper, Wyoming.

On a lark one day I visited the manager of the local Television Station. I asked him if he needed a newsman. He said "as a matter of fact I do. I only have one now and he is not very creative." He pulled out a beat-up early model Polaroid camera (it only worked with black and white film), handed it to me and said "Here's your gear—you've got the job." Upon notifying the manager of the rock and roll station of my decision to switch to television I received an urgent phone message from the owners the station. It was short and to the point "You are a traitor!"

At my new employer, I soon found myself preparing and delivering the early morning radio news, the noon hour radio news and television show, the 5pm television news, weather and sports and the 5:35pm radio news. In the evening I would write and prepare the 10 p.m. television news, weather and sports and anchor each all myself. It was a great experience and was the best education I could possibly get, talk about hands-on. Again I felt I was creating another opportunity rather than just waiting for something better to come along.

Initially when I covered a story, be it an accident, a fire, a school board meeting, or a City Council meeting I would take black and white Polaroid photos, then when back at the studio I would write the story and match photos to the text. The photos would be glued with rubber cement to plastic sheets about 12 inches square, placed in order in slots on a wooden device we hand-constructed and the camera person would physically pull the plastic sheet out of the slot quickly so the next camera shot would be the next photo.

Talk about a primitive beginning. Thinking back it reminds me of a family TV station I visited one evening in a small Wyoming town. Dad anchored the news while Mom ran a small wall-mounted camera controlled by a toggle switch, then Mom would turn on a tape recording timed to slides, advertising a local business. During that commercial Mom would be replaced at the controls by Dad while she posed herself in front of a weather board. During her weather Dad would be replaced by their son at the control board while he ran back to the anchor desk to deliver the sports news and bid all a good night. Where there is a will, there is a way.

Within a year at KTWO we were getting viewer response. We added a sports announcer and a weather girl and even another reporter. We purchased an expensive film camera and eventually even our own film processor. I learned how to operate the camera and the processor again by "hands-on" experience.

A girl I was dating who was from Chicago worked at a school for developmentally disabled children in Casper and talked me into another adventure, producing, writing, interviewing, filming, editing and narrating a thirty minute film documentary about the school. That was the first of ten television documentaries I researched, photographed, edited and narrated through my career. I completed two more in Wyoming. One was shot at the Gottsche Rehabilitation Clinic in Thermopolis, Wyoming, a rehabilitation facility for patients with traumatic head injuries. The second was at the State Prison in Rock Springs, Wyoming *"A Day in the life of a Prisoner".*

In 1960 Senator *John F. Kennedy* knocked down (politically) *Richard Nixon* to become President. In 1963, as you know President Kennedy was assassinated and his Vice President, *Lyndon Johnson* was sworn in. It was pretty much a given Johnson would win the Presidency in 1964 and for that reason, Nixon chose not to run but he did intend to seek the office in 1968. He did actively campaign in 1964 on behalf of republican candidates around the country.

One day, during the 1964 political campaign I received word Richard Nixon was planning a campaign trip to Wyoming. I was standing by with my 16 mm camera when he arrived. When he departed from the plane and moved into the terminal I was allowed to do an interview with him. I then rushed back to the car and hit the highway to Cheyenne some 180 miles away. I was hoping to arrive at the Cheyenne airport in time to catch Nixon departing again from the same plane but in Cheyenne.

Nixon and Me

Shortly after passing through the town of Douglas I was checking the clock and found I would really have to move along to arrive at the Cheyenne Airport in time. I stepped on the gas. A few minutes later I noticed in the rear view mirror a Highway Patrol car following very close. I glanced at the speedometer, I was traveling about 105 miles an hour. As I slowed down the Patrol officer went around me and waved, then seemed to disappear. I did make it and did get the footage I needed which I immediately hurried back to Casper in time to process the film for the 10pm news. I kept waiting for a reprimand from the manager who I theorized would be contacted by the highway patrolman but never heard another word about it.

When it comes to generating local news in a small town, I learned a good lesson in those early days. The best way to gain trust and get good story tips was to find out what time each day the District Attorney, the City and County officials and the political movers and shakers went to the coffee shop. At least in Casper a daily visit to the coffee shop proved invaluable indeed. The more time you spend with these potential news sources in that informal setting contributing to a (usually political) conversation, the more freely these folks talk and soon you are a trusted member of the circle. In a small town like Casper, it was easy on a slow day to generate news. I called a political news source (let's say a Democrat), then I would relate something told me over coffee by another source (a Republican) "Did you hear what he said about you?" Then I would mention to the original source over coffee about what the Republican said and we were off and running. You could keep that going for days on end.

The Casper Police Chief in the early 60s was a fellow with a great sense of humor. He liked it when new "green" reporters showed up at his desk seeking news stories. There was a somewhat colorful area of town called "the Sand Bar" that allegedly housed some "secret" all night "bottle clubs" and some traditional brothels, one that featured great steaks and music on their menu for those who weren't interested in the more obvious back room fare. The chief would suggest to new young reporters that they visit the area and report back to him if they saw anything "suspicious." Until "later years" what had been happening in the Sand Bar was basically unchanged from the early days. Today however the Sand Bar is transformed into an upscale community with newer apartment complexes, homes, bars and shops. Time marches on.

In 1909 the Platte River was diverted by construction of the Pathfinder Dam. That left a flat sandy river bottom that soon became a haven for old field workers, prostitutes, gamblers, bootleggers and shysters. It had a history in the 1920s and 30s of being a semi-permanent stopover for all kinds of strange characters. In the early 1960s the houses of ill repute were still operating, pretty much 24 hours a day. The sand bar was located on the Northwest side of the downtown and was the site for a number of houses constructed in the 1930s for basically illicit purposes.

In getting to know those folks I learned that even though their mode of earning a living may have been morally questionable, they were sincere, hard working and friendly. The food they prepared, sometimes at two or three in the morning was the best found anywhere in Wyoming.

Because the television station was located in a low population area, we were given a lot of leeway to try new things, to be creative. We attempted to produce our own children's show. We set up bleachers in the television studio. I contacted a high school friend of mine who was an actor and a character. His younger brother was in my high school class and was a varsity wrestler. I had served as the wrestling team manager and these two brothers both got a disc jockey jobs at the radio station.

I was listening to one of his on-air shifts one day as I was making my news rounds. One of the brothers came on microphone and said something like this:

> "You know folks I sit here for hours to spin these records for ya—the more I stare at that turntable spinning round and round and round while I'm sitting still, the more I wonder what would happen if the turntable didn't move and the room went round and round around the turntable. Let's give it a try—all right you guys line up and on my count push HARD!! Ya ready—on the count of 5—One . . . Two . . . Three . . . Four . . . four and a half, now get ready for the BIG PUSH—OK FIVE!!" You immediately heard a choir of men shouting OOOOF which in fact was the opening of a Pat Boone recording called the *"Wang Dang Taffy Apple Tango."*

I learned many years later that one eventually became a lawyer, then a federal arbitration judge of some type in Denver. I contacted the older brother when I worked at the Casper TV station and asked if he'd be interested in working in the newsroom in Casper and also becoming "Captain Jack" hosting a weekly children's telecast. He jumped at the chance. He became "Captain Jack." He wore a pirate costume and was ham enough to make the kids believe it. Children were bused to the studio once a week for Captain Jack's show. We'd constructed what looked like a small wooden clubhouse in the studio and when the broadcast opened the camera was focused on the door of the little shed. At the appropriate time Jack would burst the door open, jump out and shout "HELLLLO KIDS!"

One day the camera crew unbeknownst to anyone else, taped a *Playboy* centerfold on the inside of the door so that when Captain Jack shoved the door open it would fly open and the centerfold would be seen on camera. Jack caught on quickly and instead of bursting the door open and shouting, the door slowly opened only part way. Jack, a large man, slowly squeezed through the door, quickly shutting it behind him. He put his finger to his mouth and whispered "Kids—let's be really quiet—there's someone in there sleeping—don't wake them" then he proceeded with the show. He was completely unfazed and said nothing more about it.

Many, many years later I was working for the Federal Government's Animal and Plant Health Inspection Service and was assigned to manage media calls when Mad Cow Disease was discovered in Texas. I was working with a lady who was the Public Affairs Officer for the Texas Animal Health Commission. She works in Austin, Texas and one day I mentioned to her I'd once worked in Casper. She said that was her home town. I told her I'd worked at the TV station. She said she had been one of the children who'd been brought in for Captain Jack's show and she'd never forgotten the experience (but she didn't remember watching my news cast). Another of many coincidences.

During this period the Viet Nam war continued to escalate and it appeared it would be never-ending. The military draft was still law. Because I wasn't married and wasn't going to school I was expecting a draft notice any day. Three times I was ordered to board a bus for Denver taking potential draftees for physical examinations before clearing them to be drafted. Two times I was rejected because I suffered high blood pressure problems.

My landlady's sister came to Casper for a visit. Although she was at least 15 years older than I there was a definite attraction. For about two weeks we spent every free hour together. She was from Grand Rapids, Michigan. When she returned home we kept talking via telephone. I was smitten. I suggested we get married. She said no. She was older, she'd been unhappily married before and she had children.

I honestly did not feel at the time that this country had any business in a Vietnamese Civil War and I didn't buy the propaganda that the United States was simply performing a police action to maintain peace and order. With the death counts in that conflict quickly moving higher and higher I found the war very difficult to support. However I would never have refused to serve and skip the country as did many other young men. But it provided me another argument trying to convince this woman to marry me. If I was married and responsible for a family they wouldn't be so quick to draft me. Thank goodness (for today I wouldn't even recognize her if I ever saw her again and I never did) she still said no. Besides I'd already been rejected by the military twice. Surely they'd given up on me as a candidate.

The third trip on the bus to Denver I was instructed to go to a room where there was a bed and lay down for about an hour before going through the physical. Sure enough, after lying there for an hour they took my blood pressure and it was within acceptable limits. When I returned to Casper, I informed my boss that I may be leaving very soon. He immediately picked up the telephone and called the Officer in charge of the Wyoming Air National Guard. I was told by my boss that joining the Air National Guard was a more acceptable alternative because I wouldn't be drafted into a 2 or 3 year commitment. (Instead it ended up a 7 year commitment with 179 days of active duty, intentionally one day shy of the requirement of 180 days to qualify for veteran's benefits, monthly weekend drills and two weeks each summer) I took some tests and within a week I was sworn in as a member of the Air National Guard. The very day I was sworn in (it was in the morning) I received my draft notice that same afternoon in my mail.

The draft board in my home town was contacted that same afternoon and informed I'd already been sworn in. Soon I was getting ready to take a late night military flight to San Antonio Texas to begin a six week basic training program. I was ordered to board a military aircraft immediately after Christmas Day to deliver me and other recruits to Lackland Air Force Base in San Antonio, Texas.

For a few days before that I had been suffering from an infected wisdom tooth. A friend told me the cheapest way to deal with the problem was to make an appointment with a man he knew who was a retired dentist who would work on you at his house. On Christmas Eve I went to his home, was escorted to a somewhat dingy basement room in which there was a dentist's chair and equipment to administer anesthesia and two men. One man was to knock me out and the dentist who would remove my wisdom teeth. I had a somewhat painful journey to San Antonio the day after Christmas but the pain ended about the time we arrived.

At the time I found basic training an experience unlike any other. You are tossed into a barracks with a group of guys you'd never have met in any other circumstance from all kinds of places. It shakes your complacency. Suddenly you are wearing the same clothing as everyone else, you are sleeping (for very short periods) in a room with 30 or 40 other guys, sharing one bathroom, and being timed when using that facility. Your hair is sheared so you all look alike. Early in the morning you hurry into a heavy coat because outside, where you must very quickly line-up, it is very cold. You learn the true definition of the term "hurry up and wait". By afternoon you're still wearing that heavy coat but the temperature is climbing into the 80s and 90s and you are doing exercises, marching practice and running a lot.

My "Mind's eye" memories are often triggered by songs I remember. One of the "scenes" I have stuck in my head relates to one of the first nights there. We had been rushed the entire day from one site to another and although it was already dark were again standing in line waiting for our next instruction. On a loud speaker, somewhere on the grounds of the large military base the then popular song *Ferry Across the Mercy* echoed through the darkness. Feeling homesick and lonely despite the fact I was standing with fifty other guys in a long line seemed dreamlike. I don't remember what we were waiting for in that line but the scene became a permanent memory for me. I wasn't sure that there was any significance but in the pit of my stomach, listening to a song I probably would have ignored when it played on my car radio at home, I felt an undefined sense of yearning and homesickness.

It was at Basic Training I found I was not as physically coordinated as I should have been. When running through an obstacle course I would try my best but would always get singled out. However on the day of the final basic training obstacle test my drill sergeant confided he was convinced I was trying harder than any other recruit, but couldn't seem to make the required movements. More than 30 years later I would learn why.

I was diagnosed, at age 59 with Muscular Dystrophy, a genetic progressive disease for which there is no treatment and no cure. The neurologist that made this discovery asked me if I had been physically awkward through most of my life. I had been but I'd never admitted it to myself. The only experience I could recall was the trouble I encountered meeting the physical demands of basic training.

All in all however I've always felt military basic training should be a requirement for every American youngster, male and female, six weeks BEFORE they attend high school. Self discipline, physical activity and the exposure to a wide variety of humans who are required to dress, cut their hair, walk and stand alike, obey the same set of rules and programmed responses despite race or economic class, teaches the most complex lessons with the simplest methodology. For that reason it is sad the draft was eliminated. I no longer lived at home and was full-bore into a career yet at basic training I learned for the first time how to properly fold a blanket, properly make a bed and properly store clothing, shine your shoes, maintain all your belongings in an extremely small area, it's not just basic training for the military, it is basic training for living on your own. Judging from most apartments I've seen in which college age people live, it fulfills a desperate but unmet need

My radio television career resulted in my commitment to the military spreading over a seven year period from the Wyoming Air National Guard to the Idaho Air National Guard to the Colorado Air Force Reserve with the 14th Aerospace unit in Colorado Springs, Colorado. I produced public service television announcements for the Air Guard, trained junior officers at NORAD and at Ent Air Force Base in media relations, helped write news releases and the Ent Air Force Base newspaper all-in-all a gratifying and interesting experience.

Romancing

During my four—plus year tenure in Casper, I experienced serious relationships with two women and a not so serious relationship with another. My first was a young woman, blond, blue eyes and just 5'2" tall with three children, one of them a baby. She was, at the time we met, in the process of divorcing her husband. I ended up asking a friend in the legal community to represent her and I paid the tab. I purchased a house and furniture preparing for her final divorce. She agreed to marry me about the same time I was required to join the Air National Guard sending me to Texas for six weeks, followed by another six weeks of active duty in Cheyenne. Another life lesson, love can disarm your senses and trigger crazy justifications for the choices you are making.

When I returned from Texas I met my active duty requirements at the Air Force Base in Cheyenne and drove from Warren Air Force Base in Cheyenne to Casper each Friday evening, reaching Casper in time to anchor the Friday night newscast on television, then driving 40 miles out to remote oil well country to pick up my fiancé who, with her children had been staying with her aunt. We would stay in my apartment in Casper. I would work at the radio and TV station Saturday and Sunday, drive her back to the oil rig area Sunday night and drive back to the Air Base in Cheyenne. I did that for six weeks.

When I returned to Casper after being released from active duty one day sooner than expected I walked for the first time into my new house. My fiancé was there, but she was sitting naked in the bath tub with an older man, also naked whom she introduced as her "Step Father". So much for that relationship.

Next up was a beautiful girl who I really liked. She was very outgoing and had a lot of self confidence. She liked me because she said I was a "Romantic". We had a great time together. She grew up in Chicago, where her father was a security officer for the city's subway system. I was pretty shy and not real pushy when it came to making advances. We dated for about three months and one night, after we'd been dancing at a local night spot with a group of friends, we returned to the car where she nuzzled up against me and whispered in my ear "is there something wrong with me?" I told her of course not, "Then why don't you kiss me?" From then until she travelled back to Chicago to spend time with her family for the holidays we were inseparable and couldn't keep our hands off one another. I thought I was smitten.

In her absence, her best friend and roommate kept coming by my apartment saying she had promised she would look after me while my girl was gone. I apparently wasn't as committed as I thought for by the time my girl returned from Chicago her roommate and I were spending cold nights keeping one another very warm. I felt badly about that especially when the returnee presented a gift she had purchased for me in Chicago. It was a Van Cliburn Piano recording of Tchaikovsky's Piano Concerto, my favorite. Even today when I hear that music I think about her in the back of my mind (she probably thinks about me as well but I don't think I want to know what she is thinking).

The roommate and I had a relationship for a year and a half. We started arguing a lot and I decided it was time to get married or move on. We were engaged. She too was beautiful, very intelligent and the attraction we had was undeniable. We were both competitive and headstrong. She was preparing to test for her CPA and was working for an accounting company.

We did some traveling together, went to Colorado where she met my Dad, a Christmas season visit to winter-romantic Estes Park, high in the Colorado Rockies (as the snow fell lightly Christmas music was piped into the street), then to Colorado Springs to meet my grandmother, to Denver to do some partying and dancing. It was developing into a serious affair. But after 18 months it was becoming clear we still weren't on the same plain. Somewhat chagrined at breaking up with her I decided the best way to deal was to take another job somewhere else.

I successfully applied for a position in Idaho Falls, Idaho as a reporter and TV anchor. Again I made the transition on a snowy holiday night. When I got to the Tetons it was dark and it was snowing. The farther up Jackson Pass I drove, the more blizzard-like was the weather. When I reached a newly constructed ski resort area called Alpine Village it was snowing so hard I couldn't tell for sure if I was still on the road. It was time to get off the road. I checked into a room. The resort was empty due to impassable roads. I went into the bar and there was a bartender and one other patron there. She and I talked into the early morning hours. I vented my frustration at my romantic break-up and she had a similar story. I think we both felt better about the world the next day as we each went our separate ways, never to see one another again.

I had seen singer *Judy Collins* perform multiple times at a Denver nightclub called "The Exodus." There was a time, around 1960 when the club featured the best folk singers, the best dark beer and the best rye and Swiss cheese. Judy Collins had penetrating blue eyes, played a mean acoustic guitar and her song choices were compelling. Her father was a well known disc jockey in Seattle although she spent a lot of time in Colorado. She was a classically trained pianist, a child prodigy, but fell in love with interesting lyrics, turning her skills to singing and folk songs. She was fascinated with good storytelling musically, to the benefit of us all.

Another of those memory "scenes" comes to mind. One night in Denver (when I was barely old enough to get into the club) she concluded her show playing *"Malaguena Solarosa"* requiring a fiery guitar backing. I was sitting in the front row directly in front of her. That song, those long artful fingers skillfully making the guitar come alive, that remarkable clear perfect pitch voice and most of all those incredibly beautiful blue eyes burned into my brain. She later recorded a song she'd written entitled "The Blizzard" in which she told of stopping in a blizzard in the Mountains West of Denver while fleeing a relationship and after spending the night talking with the only man in the coffee shop where she took refuge and feeling much freer the next day. The similarity with my experience at the Alpine Village and the words of her song was fascinating to me.

I continued my quest for female companionship in Idaho. I met a girl who was training to be an airline stewardess. We had some pretty heated dates, then I met a girl friend of hers. Again the girl friend and I soon became engaged (I don't know why I seem to be attracted by girl friends of my girlfriend but it did happen twice). We enjoyed wine and lunches in the park and a number of picnics along mountain streams. She was about 5 inches taller than I with a great figure and blond hair. She was a telephone operator. I purchased a ring. She took a summer assignment at the phone company's Twin Falls office, so I only saw her on weekends.

One Friday night I arrived at her Twin Falls Motel for my weekly visit and noticed she was not wearing the ring at work. I asked her why and she said she preferred not to wear it at work. This led to a lengthy argument alongside a motel swimming pool, during which the ring was tossed into the pool and along with it yet another relationship. I decided at that point I was not going to get involved with any more girls, especially those with unmarried girlfriends. I was going to focus only on my broadcast career.

The News Director was a cigar chewing tough guy who had a habit of reviewing your news copy and story scripts in the wee small hours of the morning. It was not unusual for your phone to ring at 3 a.m. and when you answer you get something like "Cooper, what were you thinking?" It became a kind of boot camp experience.

I anchored one of the television newscasts each day, radio newscasts and even pulled a DJ gig each morning on the radio side. As a reporter I covered a variety of memorable and often tragic stories the first involving the rape and murder of two young girls at a well known Jackson Hole, Wyoming hotel. 12 year old Deborah and 8 year old Cynthia were asleep in their second story hotel room. A 21 year old drifter named Andrew Pixley had climbed up the outside of the building, forced open the window to the room where the girls were sleeping, raped and murdered both. When the girl's father, 39 year old Illinois Judge Robert McAuliffe went to the room to check on the girls he found Pixley lying shirtless on the floor. He physically held him down on the floor until police arrived. When news spread through the town an angry mob of 40 people gathered at the Jackson Hole Jail where Pixley was being held. Sheriffs Deputies quickly transferred Pixley to the Lander, Wyoming jail some 170 miles away to protect him. In December of 1965 Pixley was executed.

There was a home fire that killed a family of five. Yet, as difficult as that story was to cover, another emotionally disturbing story I covered in Idaho involved the tragic and brutal rape and murder of a 15 year old girl. She was killed in the recreation room in the basement of the family's home in Rigby, Idaho. I was allowed to enter the home and shoot video of the couch on which the young girl's body was found. As we were doing that the girl's grief-stricken father was sobbing uncontrollably at the top of the stairs. It was a sob I still hear in my head. Another one of those great reporter moments.

The television station also had a studio located in a downtown hotel in Pocatello, about 50 miles from Idaho Falls. There was a reporter stationed there who did a short live report during our 10 PM news. He had scheduled a one month leave and I was appointed to replace him. I would be living in a hotel, covering the local news beat and news from Idaho State University and producing that nightly report. The old Bannock hotel was fun and the food was memorable. This great hotel has been destroyed.

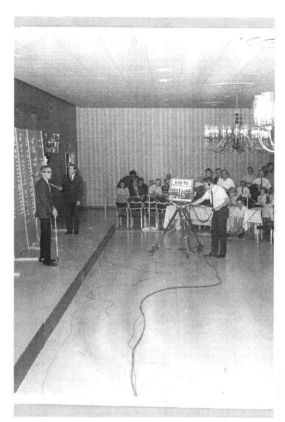

Election Night

One day I received a written note in the mail from a man who wanted me to call him and arrange a meeting at his home to discuss some "secretive" information that he thought should lead to a major local news story. Curiosity got the better of me and I did call and schedule a meeting. He and his wife greeted me. They seemed like normal people. They had a comfortable clean home. He claimed to have worked as a private detective and presented a number of documents he felt would prove local law enforcement officials were corrupt. I took copies of his documentation back to work with me, made some calls and had pretty well dismissed the allegations. About a week later there was a tip that there had been a bank robbery. A man had gone through the drive-up window of a Pocatello bank and had pulled a gun on the teller getting away with an undisclosed amount of money. When I arrived on the scene, I was greeted by this same guy, our PI with the secret documentation. At the robbery scene he saw me drive up and walked up to my car signaling me to roll down the window so we could talk. He informed me his wife was the teller who'd been robbed. He said she worked at the bank.

I talked for a few minutes to an FBI investigator and as I left I was grilled again by the so-called Private Investigator. He seemed unusually curious about what the FBI Agent told me. The next day the "P-I" and his wife were arrested and charged with the robbery. He'd driven up to the bank window, pulled a gun on his wife who quickly gave him the money. He'd parked the car and waited for the police to arrive.

While working in Pocatello the singer *Glenn Yarbrough* performed at Idaho State University. I drove to Idaho Falls and picked up my tall blond fiancé to take to the concert with me. I was a fan of the *Limelighters*; a group Yarbrough organized when he opened a small bar in Aspen, Colorado called "The Limelight". After the folk singer fad died down Yarbrough enjoyed a career as a solo performer, boosted by a hit record used for the theme song of a movie by the same name "*Baby the Rain Must Fall*". I, as usual scheduled an interview with Yarbrough and among other tidbits he told me his real love was sailing and his dream was to eventually sail around the world on a sailboat. I've read two accounts of late, one claimed he actually had two sailboats and has sailed around the world two times and another that suggested he'd owned ten sailboats and had traveled around the world five times. Which story is true I'm not sure but he did accomplish his goal, is a fine singer and I enjoyed his concert and talking with him.

Meeting a Soul Mate

I developed a friendship with the very attractive wife of our television sports anchor in Idaho Falls. She was French Canadian and would inexplicably show up at my apartment unannounced with hot food. She knew I was unmarried and had no girl friend and said she feared I wasn't eating properly. She also made it her mission to help me find a mate. Although she hadn't been living in Idaho Falls very long and didn't know too many people she did meet a single girl she thought I should meet. She said this girl was really nice, pretty cute, talked a lot but probably wasn't my type. She set up a trap, I mean a meeting over coffee. I liked the girl but she seemed a little goofy. She talked nervously and without hesitation. I asked her for a date (against my better judgment.) We went to a drive-in movie, "The Glass Bottom Boat" with Doris Day and Arthur Godfrey. Patricia Rowles really seemed sweet. She was a brunette under 5 feet tall and weighed 85 pounds. But she wasn't the type of girl I'd traditionally fallen for. She just started showing up. I'd get off the air at night and she would be at the newsroom door waiting for me. Her parents were very strict. They'd owned, at one time, 15 men's clothing stores located in Idaho, Wyoming and Montana.

The family had adopted her when she was 6 years old from a children's home in Boise, Idaho. She had two twin sisters who'd been adopted by two other families. Her sisters were older than Patricia. Their mother had actually done some work at the same children's home where she voluntarily put her three girls up for adoption.

Pat's adoption father was a Stanford graduate and one time football star who in later years was not well and rarely went out. On a few occasions we took both of her parents out to eat. He had the strangest habit of filling his pockets with free sugar packets, free matches, free napkins and anything else that was free. In the basement of their home were literally hundreds of these packets, napkins and matches safely stored away. I suspected that may have been related to his experiences during the depression years.

Handling the management and eventual sale and disposition of all of those clothing stores became his wife's responsibility. Although Pat was 24 years old, I was 25 at this time, she was required to be home no later than 11:30 PM every night. I seemed to be spending more and more time with Pat. My annual summer military commitment was coming up, meaning I had to leave to travel to the Air Guard Base in Boise where I was to spend two weeks working for the military. During that two week period I could not stop thinking about Pat. I didn't really understand why. When I returned from Boise we picked up where we left off and about two months later I asked her to marry me.

Pat was petrified at the thought (not of marrying me rather of telling her mother). I invited her mother and father to join us for dinner. During the dinner I took the bull by the horns hoping not to get gored. "Although Pat and I have only dated for three months I've ask her to marry me and she says yes." I was aware they hadn't felt I was someone Pat should be marrying. In fact her parents told her they thought I was a "four-flusher" (a 30s term for no good con man bum) She felt I had an eye on the family wealth. I waited for an explosion, I got a sputter. It was the first time I'd seen this woman at a loss for words. She forced a smile and asked "when were you thinking of doing this?" I said "We would like to have the ceremony in the next three or four weeks." She (much to my surprise) pleasantly reacted saying there was much to do. At least 200 people were invited, none of whom did I know.

I invited my mother, my father and my step mother. My step father couldn't break away at that time. As it turned out the ceremony was beautiful and touching. Thanks to an advertising "trade-out" the television station had with the Hotel Utah (the station provided advertisements to the hotel if the hotel provided an equal value of accommodations to the station's staff.) we had a marvelous three day honeymoon in Salt Lake City. We went to a French film called "A Man and a Woman" and adopted the movie's theme as our love song. Against all odds Pat and I have stayed married through the birth and raising of three children and we're celebrating significantly more than 4 and a half decades of wedded bliss.

About 2 weeks after our wedding, on New Year's Eve I was called to join the staff photographer and make a fast drive to Jackson Hole, Wyoming. I was not about to leave my new bride alone on New Year's Eve so she joined us. An annual trek up Grand Teton Peak by a famous mountain climbing instructor by the name of *Paul Petzholdt* and his students had gone badly. A winter blizzard had trapped them all for multiple nights on the peak and there was serious concern about their safety. Our photographer said he would drive.

We were to put together a story for CBS television. Problem number one, he knew a back road up the peak that would get us there faster EXCEPT blizzard conditions experienced about half-way up the mountain sent our car head-on into a snow bank with the front end of the car completely buried in the snow. He and I crawled out, grabbed a couple of tools from the back of the vehicle and started throwing what snow we could off the car. Almost on cue a highway road crew showed up and managed to pull us out and get us back on the road.

When we arrived at the location where the mountain crew was scheduled to come down, we were greeted by another highway road crew who informed us the latest word was the climbers weren't coming down for at least another two or three hours but they tipped us there had been an avalanche not too far away and there were apparently people buried in the snow. We jumped back in the vehicle and rushed off to find the avalanche site. When we arrived there we found no one was injured or buried. We jumped back in the vehicle and returned to the site where the crew was to come down from the mountain only to be greeted by another road crew who told us "Sorry, you missed them, they came down several minutes ago." They'd all come down from the mountain and had gone on into the town of Jackson Hole. I suggested we go into Jackson Hole and each of us start hitting all the bars and restaurants downtown in hopes of finding them. I went one way, the photographer went the other. Pat went into the Hotel. She found them gathered in the Dining Room, all having just sat down to a bottle of beer, waiting for a good hot meal, their first in days. She introduced herself to the "Old Man of the Mountain" himself, Paul Petzholdt and explained what had happened to us, then ran out to find me. We rushed back to the hotel.

Pat immediately asked Mr. Petzholdt if it might be possible for them to return to the side of the mountain and come back down again so we could film them finally walking into safety. Paul and his crew immediately got up, put on all their gear, went out to the vans that were carrying them and told us to meet them back at the mountain. When we arrived they were putting their gear back on and were asking us exactly where we wanted them to walk. It could not have been better. When we were done we all returned to the hotel where we joined them for dinner.

I shot an excellent interview in front of a warm fire with Paul about his ordeal. During the interview he received a phone call informing him his brother had died. I told him we should forget completing the interview we had plenty. He said no, completing the interview wasn't going to bring his brother back and apparently his brother had been ill for some time and they had expected it to happen, they just didn't know when. I was truly touched by how understanding and cooperative all of those in that mountain climbing party had been.

Years later during another media interview Paul Petzholdt best explained his reasons for devoting much of his life to the challenges of climbing mountains in the following statement:

"All my life, people have asked the question, directly or indirectly, 'Why the hell do you climb mountains?' I can't explain this to other people. I love the physical exertion. I love the wind, I love the storms: I love the fresh air. I love the companionship in the outdoors. I love the reality. I love the change. I love the oneness with nature: I'm hungry; I enjoy clear water. I enjoy being warm at night when it's cold outside. All those simple things are extremely enjoyable because, gosh, you're feeling them, you're living them, you're senses are really feeling, I can't explain it."

Paul passed away in 1999 at the age of 91. In 1965 he'd established the National Outdoor Leadership School. In 1924 when he was just 16 he climbed the Grand Teton. In 1938 he was a member of the first American team to climb K2 and he and a partner were the first to traverse the Matterhorn two times in a single day. I was also very pleased that bringing my new bride with me had paid off so well.

There were a number of times in my broadcast career that Pat's energy and honesty paid off. I was sent to Boise to do a series of interviews with members of the Idaho Legislature. There was one woman who had some clear power and tenure in the Idaho legislature who was notorious for refusing to allow reporters to interview her. In fact I was told don't even try. Pat happened to bump into her, complimented her on her hair and told her I was a reporter and she was helping me out. Pat asked her if she would take a few minutes and allow me to interview. She did, I did and others watched in awe. My boss asked her when we returned to Idaho Falls—"Do ya' think Patricia could land us an interview with Castro?" Famed interviewer *Larry King* says Castro is the only interview he was unable to get before he retired even though he pursued it for years.

A few years later Pat and I drove to Cheyenne, Wyoming so I could cover an appearance by then *Presidential candidate Ronald Reagan.* We'd checked into the same hotel where he was to stay. Pat put on her swimming suit and went out to the pool. I later came to get her and as we headed back to our room we encountered the Secret Service guys. Pat, not really aware of whom they were simply smiled said hi and "We're just running to our room" the secret service agents smiled and we kept walking. As we approached the door to our room we looked at an open door directly across the hall. Reagan was standing in front of a mirror alone, tying his tie. Pat smiled, waved and said "hi!" He smiled and said "Hi how are yah"

Once in later years I was producing a documentary at Nevada City, Montana called *"The Collector"* about Charles Bovey who collected almost everything from antique railroad cars and locomotives, to horse drawn sleighs, to horse and buggy outfits, to an enormous variety of original music machines and antique music boxes. He and his wife purchased historic buildings from all over Montana, moving them to Nevada City to help create an authentic gold rush town. The Music Hall in his town was the original Recreation Hall at the Canyon Lodge in Yellowstone National Park. It was dismantled in 1959 and moved to Nevada City where it houses the largest collection of music machines in the World.

The town, with very authentic layout and architecture was often used as a site for movie production. When we arrived there, we walked a short distance from the car, looked over a fence and actor *Jack Nicholson* was standing there. Pat smiled and waved, Mr. Nicholson smiled and waved back and kept smiling and waving at her. He was shooting the film *"Missouri Breaks"* with *Marlon Brando* the entire time we were there. Each time Nicholson saw Pat he smiled, nodded his head and waved sending her into a fit of giggles.

Big Market Broadcasting

I'd sent an application, along with a book of newspaper clippings of the variety of stories I'd covered to a radio-television station in Denver. A well known Philadelphia radio programming consultant was contracted to recommend changes to improve the radio listenership. The radio station was ranked 34th out of 34 Denver radio stations with its rock and roll format. The recommendation was to drop the existing unsuccessful music format, hire a staff of news reporters and news readers and go 24-7 with news. Although Denver offers a metropolitan area population of more than three million, it was at that time the smallest market in the nation to tackle an all-news format. I was hired as an anchor and general reporter.

Until I was hired, all the other new hires were what we called "news readers" they did not have experience in reporting and writing the news. Unlike all of the news readers most of my work history was at smaller markets, smaller communities where you had to do it all. Small rural radio and TV operations don't have enough budget or income to hire only readers. Within a month of the program change, the station was ranked number one in the morning and afternoon drive times.

The radio station studio was in the basement of the television station in downtown Denver. When I reported for work the first day, I walked into the News Director's office, put out my hand to shake hands with him. The minute my hand touched his the building jerked. There was an earthquake. He immediately ran to the newsroom to get his team busy to find out details, shouting at me to grab an empty desk and get on the phone. Talk about an officious beginning.

Pat and I had just enough money for gas to get us to Denver and we had an extra 50 bucks we hoped would get us into an apartment. Looking back now I think we were delusional. But when we arrived in Denver we spotted an "apartment for rent" sign and stopped. The apartment owner was an elderly lady who lived alone with her daughter. We told her I had a new job at the television station and we only had 50 dollars in cash. She accepted that and we moved in. That was in 1967. Today that would not be possible, 50 bucks and a handshake

I was to perform a number of functions over the five years I worked in Denver. I was an editor, supervising a newsroom staff of twenty, doing telephone interviews and editing the recordings into short sound bites and writing them into story scripts. I also "stacked the newscasts" in the proper order for thirty-minute segments. I was on the air reading news about half of my day, alternating 30 minutes on, 30 minutes off.

I also over that five-year period:

- Covered, as a "beat" reporter the Colorado State Legislature, all State offices, the Courts, and yes even the police beat.
- Covered four national American Medical Association annual meetings,
- Covered four National Governors Conferences,
- Covered the stormy 1968 political campaigns from neighborhood caucuses through the national political conventions (which included the infamous rioting at the Democratic convention

in Chicago and race riots in Miami during the Republican convention). Provided television coverage of both conventions for KBTV-Television and KARK-TV in Little Rock, Arkansas, both owned by Mullins Broadcasting. The 1968 political series was honored for Outstanding Public Affairs Reporting by the American Political Science Association.

- Anchored election night coverage for both radio and television for each of the five years,
- Produced a year-long series of film and play reviews,
- Produced 35 "mini-documentary series" for radio and television on subjects ranging from drug addiction to the death penalty, from the impact of dyslexia to skyrocketing hospital costs, from child abuse to new speed-reading discoveries.
- Infiltrated a so-called "secret" camp of naked hippies high in the mountains above Boulder, Colorado along with the television news director. That group gathered and hid high in the mountains because they were convinced the World was coming to an end. I filmed a lengthy interview with their cult leader (who was Charles Manson-like)
- Along with a cameraman was physically carried out of a University of Colorado meeting hall by members of the "Students for a Democratic Society" attending a national meeting and dumped on the lawn a total of eight times in the same afternoon.
- Covered high school riots caused when Denver school district officials attempted to bus African American and Hispanic students who lived in the economically devastated areas of town to schools located in exclusive wealthy sections of Denver and bus those more fortunate students to poor sections of town, clearly a failed effort
- Drove a boldly painted news wagon to the front door of a Black Panther headquarters building that had just been raided by police and immediately had panther members on top of the roof, the hood and surrounding the vehicle. I surveyed the damage done by police, who failed to find rifles and other fire power hidden behind wall panels they ripped open and as a result of my story won the Panther's trust for reporting the incident accurately.

- Noticed, researched, then reported on-the-air the storage of tons of nerve gas in railroad cars parked directly beneath the flight path of planes arriving and leaving the nation's 9th busiest airport. They did get moved.
- Produced a 10 part television series on hospital costs.
- Produced a 30 minute radio broadcast recorded on Colorado's death row with jail cell interviews with three death row inmates.
- Produced a series of 12 half hour Christmas Programs for radio featuring high school students discussing the commercialization of Christmas, residents of senior citizens homes discussing the same, remembering the holiday when they were young—interviews about their Christmas Holidays with a number of celebrities. Viet Nam war returnees at the amputee ward of Fitzsimmons Army Hospital, Hippy Commune residents, death row inmates and others.
- Recorded interviews for broadcast with more than 150 celebrities and political leaders.

Big City Internal Broadcast Challenges

Probably the most unusual tasks had to do with internal issues at the radio station itself. For the radio broadcasts, whenever we had a story that included a recorded sound-bite we would provide the board operator, the person who actually turned your microphone on and off, played the commercials and station IDs and played your actuality or interview inserts, a copy of the script so he or she could play the sound bite at the proper time. Each on-air news reader was eventually taught how to record interviews off the telephone then cut sound bites out and write the story with the sound bite included.

That story would be written on multiple copy paper, so when completed and the editor prepared your next newscast, copies of the sound-bite story scripts would be provided the engineer. One of our unthinking and apparently brain-dead news readers during my Editor Shift wrote a tag line (a story identifier for internal use) using a derogatory term describing the African American subject of the story.

The operator on duty happened to be a young African American College student. He saw the tag line, got up from his chair and walked out.

The next morning there were several students picketing all entrances to the radio-television station in protest. This situation continued twenty-four hours a day for about two weeks. In the long run the management negotiated an agreement that called for on-air apologies, paying the young worker's college tuition until he achieved his degree and offering to re-hire him at a higher salary.

There were security guards hired for the building to escort employees in and out of work including searches and code words. There were bomb scares and threats of violence. Competing media were feeding the fire with a lot of rumor reporting. The insensitive, careless and stupid writer was fired (with that I agreed).

About this same time period some of the radio employees were approached by a labor union and were convinced our on-air people should vote for union representation. After several failed efforts to hold an election among the workers, those favoring joining the union threatened a walk-out to force the management to support the election. That walk-out occurred. I was technically considered management so I was ordered to keep us on the air and anchor the news. I read news for ten straight hours with the only breaks being 5 minute long on-the-air network news, short sports and weather inserts and commercial breaks. That is a challenge, trying to continue to sound professional, to sound as though you are really interested in this story you've already read aloud multiple times. I've often wondered if I'd set some kind of record for continuous on-air news reading.

During my fifth year in Denver the staff was notified that the Federal Communications Commission had voted to limit the number of broadcast outlets one company could own in the same market (that policy has since been changed again). That meant the television station would be required to sell-off the radio station. The buyer, as it turned out was a company that specialized in country music programs. Our staff had a series of pow-wows over this situation, chipped in to hire our own attorney and legally challenge a change in format suggesting the public good was being better served by all-news than by country music. Considering what I believe has been a decline of objective and straight forward news broadcasting over the past twenty years or so, had that occurred today the good served the public by all-news would be a harder sell.

To make a long story short we lost

All things considered working in a larger city provided its own "rush."

It reminds me somewhat of the stunts pulled in the early days of rock radio. When I worked back in Casper there was a fad in the industry to have Deejays featured in all sorts of stunts. A Denver DJ calling himself "Pogo Pogue" earned his name by jumping on a pogo stick from Denver to Boulder in Colorado—than broadcasting for several days from high top a pole downtown. Pogue's real name was Morgan White, well known for outrageous on-air stunts. In 1961 Morgan attempted to broadcast his Rock and Roll show for 14 days from the storefront window of Zales Jewelers in downtown Denver filled with real live snakes. He was rushed to the hospital after being bitten by a water moccasin. White in later years moved to Hawaii where he and another DeeJay partnered for several years on a very popular radio comedy show. He retired in Utah. White died at the age of 86 recently in Provo, Utah.

In Casper we held a promotion where we paid a thousand dollars to the first woman to show up on the first below zero weather day in Casper on the main street wearing only a bikini. I did the interview with the winner, who happened to be a 65 year old grandmother. For George Washington's Birthday our Sales Manager dressed up like George Washington, rode a horse down main street, waving an axe in the air—then at the busiest intersection in town at 8 am, (the heaviest traffic time), with me standing in the middle of the road doing a live play-by-play, chopped down a cherry tree we'd placed in a large dirt filled bucket in the middle of the intersection. The net benefit of this exercise was hard to identify. It drew a few smiles, a lot of car horns blown by people trying to get to work upset about the delay it caused—a warning from local police and some bewildered looks from passers-by.

We also placed a train caboose with a window area cut out of the side at a local drive-in restaurant from which each Deejay was to continue broadcasting for as many hours as that person could possibly stand it. I don't remember how long I lasted, I think a couple of days and I really don't remember how many hours the winner's broadcast was but the trick sure drew people at all hours to that drive-in to get a look at the goofball announcer they were listening to on the radio.

We were desperate or insane or just a lot more creative, or perhaps a combination of all in those early days of rock and roll.

Commuting with nature

My friends at work had strongly suggested my wife and I purchase a tent and spend a weekend camping at a great site located near Central City in the mountains. We made the purchase and one Saturday morning we loaded the box holding our new tent, a camp lantern, sleeping bags and cooking utensils into the car and headed into the mountains. Three hours later, we were still driving. We'd missed the turn-off to access the camping site. It was a good thing we'd purchased a gas lantern for that could provide the light we would need to construct our tent because the daylight soon left us. After trying several side roads that looked exactly like our turn-off we spotted a secluded area. It wasn't the same spot we'd been looking for but it looked just as inviting if not better.

The first item of business was to unpack the car. I wondered if my wife had anticipated a long stay for she'd packed enough provisions for a month. Behind two piles of blankets I managed to find the lantern we'd just purchased, or at least the box in which it was located. Upon opening that box I found the lantern came un-assembled. Not being one to give up easily I pulled the needed tools out of the car's glove compartment and in the light of the car's headlights managed to get the lantern assembled. Because my mechanical ability equals that of a test monkey and the instructions read like an Air Force Missile Manual, the task took about two hours to complete. Although we were both somewhat fearful the new lantern may have been wrongly assembled and might explode or something we bravely put a match to it and sure enough and at long last there was light.

We were both getting tired as it was getting very dark so we hurriedly removed the tent and the frame from the respective boxes and spread them out on the ground. Finding no directions in either box, it appeared there was no way the frame would hold up that tent. After what seemed like an hour of verbal wrestling and with the tent, the frame, and the ground it was clear it wasn't going to work. We concluded the tent could be hooked to a tree limb and provide enough shelter until morning. We spent the next thirty minutes walking through the woods measuring tree limbs that were either too high or too low. We concluded it was not meant that we should be camping that night. The next hour we growled at one another some more while we re-packed the car. Two hours later we were back in a warm bed at home

The next day we discussed the matter rationally and decided the weekend was still in front of us and we shouldn't let the obstacles of the previous night dampen our great desire to experience camping in the Colorado Rockies. The first item of business however was to return the unworkable frame to the surplus store and retrieve our six dollars. The clerk we'd talked to the day before was expecting us and for the first time he smiled as he mumbled "I knew it wouldn't work." We spent the next two hours going from store to store looking for a tent frame made for that model. Our efforts being unsuccessful, my wife suggested we let our fingers do the driving and go home and use the telephone. After several calls we struck gold. The sporting goods store located just down the street from our home did indeed have the right model. This time we were greeted by a beaming sales clerk who instructed a helper to run down to the stock room and pick up the correct Umbrella Tent Frame. A few moments later he returned with a box tucked under his arm labeled "UMBRELLA TENT FRAME METAL." We paid the clerk fifteen dollars, (ouch) loaded the box in the car, returned home, re-packed the food, blankets and equipment and once again "headed for the hills."

This time it took only two hours to find that certain spot (we still weren't certain if it were the same spot). Once again we unloaded the car, spread out the tent and opened our new tent frame box. I could feel the blood rush to my head as my brain registered complete frustration. The UMBRELLA TENT FRAME METAL we'd received was about three feet shorter than our bargain umbrella tent required. Needless to say we enjoyed a picnic lunch and a brief walk through the woods and again decided to call it quits for the weekend.

We arrived home a few minutes after the sporting goods store down the street had closed its doors. Monday morning while I was at work my wife talked again to the clerk at the sporting goods store who assured her the situation would be righted if we would return the frame we'd purchased. That week we did just that. We traded frames and were assured we had the right one for our tent. To be certain we emptied the contents of the new box on our back yard and. constructed our tent there. It did work. The new frame actually held up our bargain tent.

The weekend came again and once more the packing ritual. By now we knew the route to our special camping spot quite well so it took only about an hour of driving. This time we even brought the family pet. We tied the dog to the nearest tree. We again unloaded the car and spread out the tent. We carefully staked out the corners of the tent then emptied the umbrella frame box. I think my feelings at that moment had reached the limits of frustration. We'd apparently left the center-top piece that holds the frame together and holds the tent up, home in our back yard. Not to be defeated again I decided to take the two hour drive back home, get the part from our back yard and return. I was pleasantly surprised to find the missing part just where we'd suspected it might be, on the lawn in the back yard. I picked it up and carried it to the car and started back to our campsite (feeling something like the frontier scout bringing home the prey for food.)

My wife, while I was gone managed to improvise a tent made from blankets just in case. We did manage to construct our bargain tent so it at least resembled a tent. Darkness soon set in so we settled down for an evening of relaxation and maybe a few songs around the campfire. We had been told by friends that is the proper thing to do in this situation. After using all the matches we'd brought with us, we succeeded in lighting the camp fire. My wife, in true frontier spirit cooked a delicious hamburger, corn-on-the-cob, and pork-n-beans dinner after which we roasted marshmallows. We spent a romantic hour or two by the campfire under the stars feeling at last we were free of frustration.

Before we settled down for the night in our tent, my wife insisted we bring the dog inside the tent to sleep with us in case it rained. She also expressed the concern we might get an unwanted visit from one of the native Black Bears. It seems I'd just dozed off to sleep when I was rudely awakened by my wife's nudging and the dog's whines. "I don't know what's wrong with her she must think there's something out there!" whispered my wife in my tired ear. I mumbled something like "There's nothing out there so let her yip and go back to sleep." "Well if you won't look then I will, I'll bet it is a bear." said my wife. "If you're going to make a big deal out of this I'll get up and look" I said, "but remember its four o'clock in the morning and even bears sleep."

Bravely but stupidly, I peeked out the tent flap, listening and trying not to breath too hard. Then I heard a sound that sent a jolt through my body that quickened my breathing, pushed the blood to my tired brain and made my knees shake. Our visitor was indeed a very large Black bear. The dog now was barking and pulling to get out of the tent. I told Pat to try to quiet her down. If we are quiet perhaps it will just leave. The bear's grunts and growls were getting very close to our tent. We literally froze.

A few minutes later silence gratefully prevailed. I again peeked out and our visitor had left. "Let's get out of here fast" I said in full voice. Pat didn't answer, she was already folding up the blankets in the tent. We quickly tore the tent down and shoved everything including the dog in the car.

We arrived home about six o'clock that morning and fell into bed. About noon we awoke and looked at what had happened almost as though it were some kind of a dream we'd shared. We still were not willing to surrender. We decided to spend our Sunday afternoon right back at that same spot. At least we could enjoy a picnic lunch and a hike. When we arrived again it was cloudy and looked like rain but there weren't any bears in sight. I quickly gathered wood and two matchbooks later was still struggling to get a fire going. It was starting to rain but very lightly. "If you can't get it started let me do it 1" said my wife using her most disgusted tone. Male pride would not allow me to accept her help.

The rains came pouring down. We were being drenched. I attempted to move the car close so we could throw the blankets, utensils, cameras etc. more easily into the car. It was becoming very muddy. It was so muddy the car wouldn't move. I jammed it into reverse and stepped on the gas, shifted back to drive stepped on the gas and again in reverse until I managed to dig the tires in so deeply the mud was up to the axel. My wife said nothing, just gave me that (I pity you stupid) look that only wives can give.

I was not going to lose my temper. My feeling of frustration was reaching a level of numbness. Getting soaked to the gills I tried to dig the car out by placing an old blanket under the rear tires to no avail so I shoved some old boards beneath the drive wheels but the car was not budging. Pat and I sat in silence for about fifteen minutes. That silence was finally broken by my wife who said "I shouldn't say this dear but do you remember when we drove off the main road and down the hill, I strongly suggested you not go there? Guess what, I TOLD YOU SO!"

It was at this temper-breaking moment I heard a welcome sound. It was the sound of a four wheel drive vehicle coming down the same cow path we were on. A soft-spoken man, looking somewhat like a lumber jack pulled up and rolled down his car window. He yelled "it looks like you're stuck." I could only smile and shake my head. Without a word the man jumped out of his vehicle and pulled out a jack. He jacked up the back of my car about a foot and pushed. In a period of three minutes my car was free.

As I drove back to the main road I noticed the sun coming out, the rains were stopping. I looked at my wife who was still sitting in silence with that certain "told-you-so-but-I'm-not-going-to-say-it-again" look on her face. We were half way home when I told Pat, we have to go back. She angrily asked "Now what?"? I calmly said "we left Majorina (our dog) chained to a tree".

The next week, when all had returned to normal, while my wife was at the hairdresser, I picked up the telephone. I had made a decision. I would place an ad in the local newspaper. The ad would read "FOR SALE CHEAP: Umbrella Tent, with Metal Frame, with camping gear".

More Births

Somewhere in the midst of all of this my wife announced she was pregnant. It was fortunate she had befriended a woman who lived across the street who was the mother of 8 children. She managed to keep my frequently high strung wife calm and answer a lot of the questions Pat confronted her with on a daily basis. I was obviously keeping extremely busy and wasn't able to offer much in the way of comfort and especially expertise. I bought a book that at the time was the baby bible for new parents, written by Dr. Spock (no relation to the Star Trek character).

We also had a pet dog, when we first obtained the puppy we named it "Major" but when the puppy grew up and got pregnant we changed the name to "Majorina". I came home from work one evening to find my wife, who was 8 months pregnant at the time, crawling underneath our bed trying to help our pregnant dog deliver what turned out to be 6 beautiful puppies.

On a freezing snow covered October 7, 1969 I became a father with the birth of Troy Thomas Cooper. He joined our world at Swedish

Hospital in the Denver suburb of Englewood. He was our first of three and needless to say the birth of a child (especially the first) is indeed life altering. On that particular day 36 babies were born at that same hospital. The doctor visited me in the waiting room proclaiming "They're popping babies like popcorn back there". A nurse told me they had to place Troy in a dresser drawer until they could find an empty crib.

Late in 1971, I was contacted by a man who'd been the Sales Manager at KTWO-TV in Casper at the time I worked there. He told me he was now the General Manager of a television station in Billings, Montana and the state of Montana was beginning to organize a Constitutional Convention. Delegates, none of whom could be office holders or politicians, would be elected to gather at the State Legislative Chamber and for nearly a year would work to rewrite the State's Constitution.

Voters in Montana were asked to elect 100 delegates, none of whom could be elected or government officials. They were to convene in the State Legislative chambers to re-write Montana's State Constitution. There were basically two television groups with stations in each population center in Montana and they needed someone experienced enough to cover the convention for one of those groups for a year. I told them I was definitely interested.

We decided to call my service *"Capitol Television News"*. I would office at the small television station in Helena owned by former Montana Governor Tim Babcock. One station donated a very large and heavy film camera that had been a 35 millimeter used for commercial movie making but was converted to 16 millimeter for television use. I was provided a tripod for the camera, but no lights. A battery pack was provided. I would film reports, commentaries and interviews daily in Helena, then put the film on a bus to Great Falls. The Great Falls Station had a film processor—they would process the film then put it on a bus back to Helena (this was just prior to the development of portable video). I would edit the film then put it on a bus back to Great Falls where the completed film piece would be transferred to two-inch video tapes. The tapes would then be bussed from Great Falls to each station, Helena, Missoula, Butte, Kalispell and Billings.

Me Editing Film

What I hadn't really counted on was the Montana weather. The first film piece I produced was shot at a controversial land fill in the mountains. I was shooting myself (I would take a music stand, adjust it to the same height I was, place it where I would be standing, set the camera, turn the camera on, walk to the music stand—knock it out of the way, do my introduction then walk around behind the camera and turn it off then repeat the process for the next scene). The temperature that day was nearly 40 below zero. I started carrying my wife's heaviest coat to wrap around the camera to keep it from freezing up.

Interviews that weren't done at the TV studio in Helena would have to be filmed outside because we had no lights. I would visit the Governor daily, at that time it was Forrest Anderson. He would put on his coat, gloves and winter hat and follow me outside to film the interview. I remember toward the beginning of the constitutional convention filming a presentation by the governor. I brought Patricia to help me carry equipment and I warned her to be ready to grab the camera if it slipped. The tripod I had did not have wheels or locks or rubber pads and when it was set up on a smooth waxed floor, as it was this day, it tended to slide. Just as the Governor started speaking to the new delegates, the camera took a slide—I told Pat "whatever you do hold onto the camera don't let it fall"—She replied "But one of the points is sticking in my foot and I'm holding the camera and the sliding tripod and I may go down with the camera—" My response "Just don't drop the camera!" Afterward Patricia, nursing some scrapes on her legs and feet told me "I saved the damned camera but did you care about the injuries your wife might be suffering?"

I covered the state offices and the Constitutional Convention for one year. After the narrow win in that June election, equally narrow court decisions and state and federal affirmations, the new Constitution was approved. As soon as the constitutional dust settled, the station managers gathered in Helena to make a decision on continuing the service and funding the costs of proper equipment or give it up. Dale Moore, a flamboyant broadcaster who owned twelve radio and eight television stations in 4 states and in Puerto Rico attended the meeting. He favored ending Capitol Television News with the conclusion of the convention. The other managers agreed but before the meeting was adjourned they praised the work I'd done and Mr. Moore asked me to consider becoming the News Director/Anchor for Western Broadcasting's properties in Missoula, Butte and Kalispell. I accepted.

Pat, my son Troy, our dog Majorina and I had been living on the side of a mountain, about 20 miles outside of Helena, Montana in a double-wide mobile home sitting on 12 acres complete with a number of outbuildings. There was one home close enough for its occupants to be considered "neighbors". It was occupied by a young couple. He worked for the Montana Fish, Game and Parks Division. His specialty was birds. He kept a variety of birds in cages in his home including a falcon and a golden eagle.

At Christmas time he and his wife flew back to their native New York City for two weeks and he asked Pat if she would be sure his birds were cared for. He left instructions telling Pat that in the freezer there was a collection of frozen rodents to be fed to the birds. Pat was to pull the rodent out, allow it to thaw then place it in the bird's cage. Pat said she had to do that quickly or they would consume her fingers with the rodent.

We gave Majorina to another neighbor who ranched about a mile away. He and his wife had 8 children and asked if they could have our dog for their children. We, of course were attached to Majorina, but it would be easier to find a home to rent in Missoula without a pet and we knew she would be well cared for with that many playmates. We said our goodbyes to our neighbors and their birds, loaded up a rental truck and headed for Missoula. We were fortunate, or so we thought, to find a completely renovated Victorian style home to rent. We had an extra room on the main floor and the second floor had been made into a large apartment. We would agree to pay full rent and were allowed to sub-lease the apartment to make our rent affordable. The upstairs residents were students at the University of Montana. There were four very tall, very country boys from farmsteads around the Dillon area. There was also a nursing school nearby and in a short time young female nursing students started showing up (like a moth to the flame) and the parties began.

The house was adjacent to the river that ran through town and soon our roof became home to a group of roof rats. We could hear the rats at night through our ceiling. When we ventured up to the boys apartment to investigate we learned they were using an attic area, with a small half-size door to their kitchen as a garbage dump—still-wet food and meat included. For the river rats it was a paradise, warm and lots of food. When confronted, the boys politely acknowledged they should not be doing that, promised to clean it up and said the rats were no problem. Not thirty minutes later one of the boys came down the stairs to show me the huge rat he had nailed with his bowie knife, still jammed in the animal's body. Only in Montana.

My first day working in Missoula happened to be Election Day. During a live lunchtime television broadcast, the local host told his co-host "you know we've got a Native American Indian running for governor and he's had a felony conviction how is it that he can't vote because of his felony conviction but he can still run for office?" I immediately received a call from the candidate's campaign manager threatening to challenge the outcome of the state's gubernatorial election because the comments were aired while people were voting. Welcome to Missoula.

As it turned out Missoula had a very diverse group of residents ranging from the left-leaning environmentalist to far-right lifetime multi-generational Montana conservatives.

Today young people enjoy referring to Missoula as a "community of hippies" which is not really a valid description. I think long-term residents prefer being tagged as "conservative and fiercely independent." Having seen and reported on the whole hippie era, I feel today's generation really has little understanding of that "make love, not war" generation. While this country's lengthy and bloody involvement in the Viet Nam war fueled mass protests, the "hippy" movement seemed more driven by the backlash to the social and sexual repression of the 50s and the growing fascination with psychedelic drugs. Exploitive movies, media coverage (for the first time in history we saw on TV the bloody reality of war right in our living rooms nightly) helped fan the flames of what appeared to be a weakening moral code among many younger Americans. Rebellion, exploitation and a growing distrust of our political leaders boiled over in the 60s.

Another very interesting character I befriended in Montana was an extremely intelligent young man who had spent a number of years in Chicago training to be a Priest. He'd become discouraged with the church's teachings and married a young lady he met at an anti-war protest. She had intended to become a Nunn but fell in love. They produced two beautiful girls and decided to move to the remote mountains of Montana. Although he had no broadcast experience his knowledge and intelligence proved an asset as a reporter and as a writer. He anchored our television weather segments, worked as a general assignment reporter and wrote interesting reviews of new films and plays. We became very good friends.

One summer day he went hiking in the Montana high country, an experience he considered to be very spiritual. The evening after he returned home he came down with an extremely high fever. Doctors had a difficult time diagnosing the problem. Two days after entering the hospital he was dead. He was only in his early 30s. The final diagnosis was tick fever. He was buried, with permission granted by the National Park Service, high on a mountain peak in a very private and limited service. There was an area on the edge of Missoula called Rattlesnake Creek Park. I felt so badly about his sudden death I found myself walking alone along Rattlesnake creek thinking about him, his life and the loss of a wonderful father (he and his wife had two girls, each pre-school age.) husband and friend.

Another scene that triggers a memory even today: I remember walking one day across the University of Montana campus with my wife and his wife and their two small daughters when a young man riding a bicycle passed. He was naked. These were the days of hallucinogenic drugs and streakers so it really wasn't surprising. One of the children walking with us asked her Mom "Why is that man naked?" She nonchalantly replied "He's going to go take a bath" to which the little girl responded "oh."

There was a young man who worked at our television station and I don't honestly remember his name. He was very talented, working lighting, set design and even as a director during live broadcasts. He was soft spoken, clean cut and looked like a boy you really would have no concerns with if he were dating your daughter. One day he simply disappeared. He didn't show up for work. His friends had no idea where he was.

Many years later I was producing a television news feature on the so-called "Rainbow Family". They were a group of people who pretty much adopted an independent hippy-like lifestyle. They raised their own food developing vegetable gardens, milk from animals etc. They lived commune style and they would simply move with some frequency, usually walking for transportation. I recognized this young man among them, although I did not get the opportunity to talk with him. A major magazine later did a story on this rambling group and in one of the photos I again recognized this young man. At that point he had been with that group for a number of years. Inexplicable but it does raise questions that perhaps our wants, desires, moral boundaries and beliefs are not a one size fits all. We may be walking to the beat of our own familiar drum but to others it's not the same beat. Today, 30 years later Rainbow Families still thrive throughout the country including here in Montana.

We lived in a few different rental properties over the five years or so I worked in Missoula in the 70s. When our second child arrived we needed to find an apartment with an extra bedroom for the baby. The new arrival was a boy we named "Travis". Our first child was a boy we named "Troy" We felt our boys should have good masculine old West type names. I nicknamed Travis "Mr. Me Too" for as a tot he'd rush after his older brother proclaiming "Me Too." We moved to an apartment that was adjacent to a golf course on a mountainside facing the city (doesn't sound real "ole West"). We quickly became accustomed to golf balls smashing into a sliding door at the back of our apartment. Our apartment was also built over the home's garage so we had to become accustomed to exhaust fumes from a motorcycle the owners son fired up every morning. During the snowy winter months the golf course made a great winter play land for our boys

One Sunday evening I received a telephone call from famed zoologist *Merlin Perkins*, the host and creator of the long running television program *Wild Kingdom*. Perkins said he, his producer Don Meier and cameraman Ron Pinney were staying in a motel in Polson and planned to shoot a segment the next day about the Bighorn Sheep living on Wild Horse Island located on Flathead Lake Wild Horse Island was initially used by the Salish Kootenai Indian Tribe to hide horses protecting them from being stolen by other Tribes. It is home to a number of wildlife, including bald eagles, Bighorn Sheep, mule deer and Coyotes among others. The island is 2100 Acres and accessible only by boat.

Merlin said a small plane would be used to roundup and move the sheep and their cameraman would be shooting film from the air but he asked if I would help by shooting film of the sheep on the ground. I met the crew Monday morning at 4 am in below zero weather. We boarded a small boat and landed on the Island. I was positioned behind a blind and when I heard the plane coming toward me I was to film the sheep running towards me, past me and behind me. It wasn't difficult but it required hours of waiting in the cold.

When we had what we needed we returned to the motel where Merlin pulled out a bottle of bourbon and we spent a couple of hours warming and becoming acquainted. That show aired from 1962 through 1988.

Perkins died of cancer in 1988.

My sons clearly remember one very cold winter evening when a public grade school building caught fire. I had my two boys with me when I got a call on the two-way radio in my car about the fire. I rushed directly to the fire, told the boys to wait in the car, grabbed the camera and ran off to shoot film. At this time the entire building was engulfed in flames. When I felt I'd covered the blaze adequately, I returned to the car but the boys weren't there. I started to panic, thinking the worst. What if they tried to follow me to the fire itself and were injured. As I walked back toward the fire I passed one of the police cars parked at the scene and happen to notice sitting in the back seat were my two sons. The police officer came over to me telling me the boys jumped out of my car and were headed to the fire to find me when he spotted them and ordered them to stay in the car. To this day the boys remember the incident and remember how frightened they were thinking they were being arrested and hauled off to jail.

Although we were living in a fisherman's paradise I hadn't done much fishing in the past. I'd done some lake fishing in Kansas and with my grandfather on my mother's side in Colorado and as a child had hunted rabbits and pheasants with my Dad. I was far from being an outdoorsman. We befriended a couple living in our new Montana neighborhood. He was an avid outdoorsman and challenged me to go fishing with him. I agreed. He didn't tell me I would be riding on the back fender of a dirt bike (motorcycle) and each time we'd hit a bump in the many miles of pathways he called "routes" I would fly off the bike landing with a thud on my backside. When we finally reached our destination it was picture post card perfect. No humans for miles—a sparkling blue water lake with fish jumping everywhere out of the water. In his backpack he carried a tubular blow-up boat, folded ores, fishing gear and even gourmet meals to which you just add water and cook over a portable fire. I still marvel at the amount of stuff he'd packed away in that backpack. I wasn't much on fishing but I've got to admit I'd never seen a place like this. You'd toss your line in the water and almost immediately you would pull out a beautiful trout. It didn't require much time to catch our legal limit. It was a memorable experience but my back and my backside found great relief in stretching out on the couch in our apartment again. That was a remarkable day but it was my last outdoorsy adventure.

I covered and had the freedom to comment on or about nearly every type of story during my years in Missoula. There was the tragic disappearance of 7 year old Susan Jaeger who was abducted from a tent in which she was sleeping during a family camping outing at the Missouri Headwaters State Park at Three Forks. I visited the camp scene and filmed a report. I ended my news broadcast the night that report ran with a commentary expressing the sadness and anger most of us felt about the tragic incident. On the eve of her abduction one year later, Susan's mother Marietta received a telephone call from a person who told her he was the perpetrator of this horrible crime. He apparently intended to taunt her. Instead of anger, she expressed compassion for him, keeping him on the telephone for over an hour. From that conversation she was able to provide enough personal information about him that FBI investigators were able to create a profile that led to his arrest. It reportedly was one of the first arrests related to what was then a new technique used by the FBI that involved developing a profile identifying the characteristics of a person most likely to commit the crime. The killer was identified as David Meirhofer of Manhattan, Montana. He was 23 at the time. He later admitted her murder and abduction as well as the abduction and murder of 19 year old Sandra Smallegen whom he'd once dated, and two other boys 12 year old Michael Raney and 13 year old Bernard Poelman. Meirhofer, in September of 1974 committed suicide while being held in jail.

Around the same time period little Susan was abducted and murdered another Missoula child was abducted from the sidewalk in front of her Missoula home. She was 5 year old Siobhan McGuiness. Her body was found the next day stuffed into a culvert beneath a highway about ten miles East of Missoula. That incident is still being investigated. The crime occurred in 1974 and the investigation was re-opened in 2008 after DNA samples were taken. Both of these stories were difficult for me to report. I had a new baby boy and a 5 year old boy at home and these heinous crimes committed on children to me represented the absolute worst type of crime imaginable.

On Law Day of that year, a day to recognize the contributions of American Lawyers, supported by the American Bar Association, I reminded my viewers on my nightly commentary "One Man's Opinion" that Richard Nixon was a lawyer. That commentary led to receipt from the Montana Foundation at the University of Montana of an award naming "One Man's Opinion" the Television Program of the year.

There were many moments working in Montana it was an experience like no other. In terms of scenes that became memories I remember then Montana Governor Tom Judge invited me to join his group and shoot video on a helicopter tour of areas hit hard by a winter blizzard. When we landed in Cutbank the turbulence from the helicopter's propellers blew blinding snow all around us. When the snow cleared we saw hills and mountains of snow 6 to 10 feet high. I was trying to get useable film footage but having to wait for the helicopter engines to be completely shut down first.

I remember being invited by Governor Judge to a party for movie crews filming scenes for producer *Charles Pearce* who produced two movies in the Flathead Lake-Kalispell areas. At the party I sat beside *Dawn Wells*, better known as Mary Ann Summers, the cute brunette on Gilligan's Island. I watched wonderful veteran character actor *Elisha Cook* sit by himself in a corner sound asleep at each of three parties my wife and I attended. I had a truly interesting conversation with the late *Denver Pyle*, who played Doris Day's father on the *Doris Day television series*. He was also a good friend of hers which fascinated me because I'd been a huge fan of hers since childhood.

I remember boarding a commercial flight from Missoula to Denver on the same plane the camera crew filming the movies boarded. One of the film crew had picked up and was carrying with him three tiny new born wild mountain lions he wanted to take home to Los Angeles. Can you imagine today trying to get three live lion cubs through security?

Dale Moore—a respected broadcaster, businessman and entrepreneur

Dale Moore owned and operated KGVO Radio-Television in Missoula as well as KTVM in Butte and a Satellite television station in Kalispell. He owned, as I'd mentioned earlier several radio and television operations including a television network in Puerto Rico. At the time I worked for him he'd invested in a polled Hereford livestock operation located on a ranch near Missoula where he'd recently constructed a large 8 bedroom home. He had an award winning Polled Hereford steer that was the largest bull I'd ever seen. He'd won best of show ribbons at the National Western Livestock show in Denver and I remember shooting film one day as the bull, "Big Sky Guy" was paraded into the Brown Palace hotel in Denver and was led into and up the elevator to the top floor for a party Dale was hosting at which "Guy" was the star attraction. Dale's life ended tragically when he and his young pilot were killed when his private plane smashed into a mountainside.

One day I received a tip that the earthen dam on the Snake River in Idaho had collapsed and it was sending floodwaters down the river toward the city of Idaho Falls. When I informed Dale Moore he immediately contacted his pilot and told me to go to the airport quickly and the pilot and I would head for the catastrophe. We flew over the dam and shot film, then down the Snake River. We saw large gatherings of people alongside the river and decided to land to film some interviews. The gatherings were people waiting to watch the crest hit. It was predicted to hit the area where all of these bystanders were within an hour. Several families were sitting on the bank of the river having picnics waiting to see the flood crest. I interviewed a few of those folks asking if they weren't fearful that when the crest hit they may not easily escape. Most responded they felt there would be plenty of time for them to flee. I didn't hear of any fatalities but the attitude and the daring of these people has puzzled me for years. Was it bravery or stupidity?

One day I was summoned to Dale's office where he asked me to consider producing a one hour television documentary about the coal strip mining operation in Eastern Montana.

Dale had recently purchased a nine passenger aircraft and had added a young pilot to his staff. It was the same plane that in later years would take his life. Dale, KGVO Manager Lynn Koch and I flew to Billings to make initial contacts and assess what we would need to do to get started. Visually it was extremely interesting for the mining equipment used was gigantic. Parking a large full size pick-up truck beside one of the huge diggers made the pick-up appear to be a small toy. I would be my own photographer, would do the interviews, write the script, edit the film, narrate and anchor the broadcast, it would be my project.

The first night we were in Billings was the first time I'd ever visited that city. Remember this was in the early 1970s and much of the city's colored past was still evident. Dale, Lynn and I visited a bar in a historic downtown hotel that featured an older woman who performed great and hilarious bawdy songs. It was to me like something from an old western movie. A drive around the lower downtown area disclosed a section comprised of one room structures with picture windows in which ladies of the evening would sit and beckon you to join. They were appropriately tagged "the cribs" and their purpose was obvious. One of the mayors to be elected a few years later abolished the cribs and cleaned up the downtown but when you bring up the history to long-term Billings residents they were happy to see them go but most agree "The Cribs" provided colorful memories of the City's checkered past.

The first place to visit in planning my production was the town of Colstrip. At that time there were a number of brand new homes in Colstrip. In fact to me it appeared the coal interests owned and built their own community with most of the residents working for "the company". I've since learned the town was first established way back in 1924. Its primary industry has always been coal mining and electricity production. The Northern Pacific Railway actually established Colstrip to house workers operating an "open" strip mine to produce coal to fire the railroad's steam engines.

In 1958 the railroad switched to diesel engines and the mine was shut down. The mine was purchased a year later by the Montana Power Company. In the 1970s, (when I took an interest) the Power company announced the mining operation would resume operations to feed coal fired electrical plants the company proposed building During the construction of the power plants through the 1970s and early 80s Colstrip became a "boom town" of sorts explaining all the new home building that was occurring there at the time.

In 1968, just a few years before my visit, there were only 100 residents, by 1980 there were more than 1500. The population peak climbed to 7500 in 1982, by 1990 the population had dwindled back to a little over 3-thousand. When I last checked the population stabilized at around 2400.

The reason this captured the attention of Dale Moore was the belief he had that this type of development could eventually give a boost to the Montana economy. There was a growing and sometimes angry debate, especially in Missoula, about the environmental aspects of the strip mining. There was a regulation enacted by the Montana legislature in the heat of this debate that all land cut-up by the immense machinery used, would have to be restored to its original state so there would be no visible signs in later years of strip-mining.

While Dale Moore wanted me to be objective he definitely wanted clear video of ground that had been mined being returned to it's "before" state, providing visible proof the land would be fully restored. To balance the report it was suggested I contact a Colstrip area rancher whose property line was adjacent to some of the development. His name was Wally McRae. He ran a 30,000 acre cattle operation, the "Rocker Six Cattle Company Ranch" on Rosebud Creek just south of Forsyth. Mr.

McRae, who did not approve of much of the activity, was willing to talk.

At that time McCrae would have been in his early 40s. He projected the image of the perfect rancher. Mr. McRae was friendly, informative and responsive. He drove me around his ranch, talking about his land and that project. He allowed me to film a lengthy and truly interesting interview with him relaxing in a lawn chair with some of the best scenery on his place clearly visible in the background. He was direct, honest and impressive. He provided a list of clear objective arguments, so clear and direct I really didn't need any others to honestly balance my report.

Years later, when I was working as an agricultural broadcast journalist in California (a farm broadcaster) I befriended a woman who was a great fan of cowboy poetry. In 1984 she'd attended what was billed as the first gathering of "cowboy poets" and she said she'd been especially impressed with a poet by the name of Wally McRae. That was the first time I'd associated McCrae with anything but ranching. I later learned when he was in school in Colstrip McRae was involved in theater and had written and collected his poems for a number of years, finally taking a boot-box full of his poems to a writer at the Billings Gazette who helped him get a book of his poems published. He's now published three or four books of his poetry. He'd acted in community theater groups, had written, directed and acted in plays and even sang in a barbershop quartet. He'd received, in 1990, the National Endowment for the Arts Heritage Award, an award also received by another friend and acquaintance of mine I'll write more about later in this effort the famed Hispanic singer, musician entertainer Lalo Guerrero. McRae also connected with another person I'd met and became friends with during the years I worked in Montana, the late CBS television journalist Charles Kuralt.

Kuralt was famous for his "On the Road" series of interviews with people all across the United States. He'd taken time in Missoula to appear on my television broadcasts and I'd talked with him a number of times via telephone. He was always seeking ideas for stories and interviews in Montana. Kuralt talked about his interviews and discussions with Wally McRae in his book *Charles Kuralt's America*.

Kuralt was genuine, creative and a great broadcaster. He'd purchased and restored an old school building located along the Big Hole River in Montana with an eye toward eventually writing and retiring there. However he passed away from Lupus Disease when he was 62.

Every night, five nights a week I would end my television broadcast with a commentary I called "One Man's Opinion". The mail that commentary generated was heartwarming to me. Viewers, even if they disagreed with me would write to tell me so but also comment on how much they enjoyed that section of the broadcast. People would call me, sometimes in the middle of the night at home to discuss a point I'd made on my broadcast. I found the reception and the response consistently gratifying.

I was also given the opportunity during my Missoula career to produce a documentary about Child Abuse that was used for social study classes at the University of Montana. I also produced a series of four hour-long television programs supported by a grant from the National Endowment for the Arts, written by the Missoula Historical Society. This kind of freedom is what made working in smaller markets far more interesting to me.

Chapter Four

Learnin' Country Talk

I received a call from a friend who was managing a radio station in Scottsbluff, Nebraska and he wanted to know if I'd be interested in partnering with him and the radio station's owner to create a farm radio network. We would provide up-to-the-minute market reports thirteen times a day with the broadcast originating in Nebraska. I would also be asked, for a while anyway, to anchor the morning news at KOLT in Scottsbluff and fill-in on the announcing shifts as needed.

He wanted my wife and I to meet him at the Denver airport, then he would fly us (he had a plane and a pilot's license) in a small plane from Denver to Scottsbluff so we could look over the town, the radio station and do some talking about farm broadcasting. My wife was pregnant at the time with our third child. It was a very hot summer day and the small craft hit every hot air bump it could find between Denver and Scottsbluff. Patricia had turned a bit "green" by the time we landed.

We would be one of the first networks to serve Western Nebraska. There were other stations in Nebraska and Colorado that had expressed an interest in the service. "But," I suggested "I'm not a farmer—I'm a broadcaster. I couldn't tell you what hundredweight or futures numbers actually meant" I was assured that was no problem. The prospect of owning one-third of any business sounded inviting to me so I agreed.

I was to spend the first six weeks virtually camped out at the University of Nebraska Research facility in Scottsbluff learning all I could about farming. I would actually be broadcasting from a commodities brokerage house in Scottsbluff equipped with a big trading board and teletype updates. I spent some prep time with the agents teaching me the mechanics of the futures markets and how "hedging" worked and what local farmers were most concerned with. When I hit the air I felt far more comfortable with the task at hand, although being responsible for producing and airing a live broadcast via telephone lines to what turned out to be twelve radio stations located in Nebraska, Wyoming, Colorado and Kansas.

To help us sell time in our broadcasts to national advertisers we contracted with a man from Texas, who specialized in selling national agricultural advertising agencies farm broadcast air time. He asked that I join him on a couple of his trips to Kansas City, Milwaukee and Chicago to call on advertising companies that created and placed advertising for farm implements and farm chemicals. He asked that I wear cowboy boots and a hat and not sound too "northern".

His sales pitches focused on talks with the advertising account executive about that person's family life, funny stories and a very brief reference to renewing their contract for another year. He said the only time they liked to talk business is when it is time to prove to the client their advertising buys were working. Our network allowed the individual stations to sell one commercial in each broadcast and sponsorships. We would sell the other two and that would provide our income.

We started off pretty well. Listenership and response was positive. We hired a Farm Broadcaster from Lubbock, Texas to sell advertising time on our network in our region. I was asked to join an organization called the National Association of Farm Broadcasters. I applied, paid the fees then arranged to meet our National sales person in Kansas City at the annual meeting of this group. When I arrived at the lobby of the hotel I could not believe what I saw. Every seat in the lobby was filled by guys, most in cowboy hats, with tape recorders in hand interviewing one another.

I would attend 5 or 6 of these annual gatherings, always held at the same hotel. The annual meeting was originally scheduled to coincide with the National Future Farmers of America annual conference and with the American Royal Parade, Rodeo and Livestock Show. In later years the wind was taken from the event when the FFA conference was moved.

Because I'd reported on politics and won a few awards for that coverage didn't necessarily mean I would be a politician. Nonetheless my partners in "Agribiznet" (The agreed upon name for our new network) thought I should immediately start lobbying to get myself elected as President of the NAFB. To them the logic was clear. National agricultural advertisers would be sure to buy the programs anchored by the NAFB's President. My lobbying efforts fell flat.

The first farm broadcaster I asked to nominate me for the position informed me that this was a job you did not politic for. There were members who'd been farm broadcasters for many years and I was a "newbie" to this farm stuff. I did get nominated but was never selected for an office.

This annual affair featured hosted party rooms throughout the hotel open most of the night. Our group, (our national rep and our local area sales exec) formed a little club. We would gather in the lobby bar at the hotel opening day, and tell tall tales over very smelly cigars. Just recently while surfing the internet I found a 15 minute video featuring our salesman, who apparently after the break-up of the Nebraska Agribiznet returned to his home town in Texas. On the video he talks about farm broadcasting and the changes he'd seen in farm broadcasting over his 25-30 years as a farm broadcaster for the Lubbock radio station KRFE.

Through the National Association of Farm Broadcasters I met several folks whose names I was somewhat familiar with including Orion Samuelson (I later learned he was considered the "Grand PooBah of Farm Broadcasters") from Chicago and the Denver broadcaster I'd listened to as a child Evan Slack.

We were tasked with taking a journey, along with a Denver radio salesman named Van Kyrious who was once our production director in Denver. We were to drive through Kansas and Iowa attempting to sign up additional radio stations to broadcast our program and share advertising availabilities.

Mentioning Van Kyrious reminds me, I remember, during my Denver broadcasting days commentator Paul Harvey would, with some frequency deliver his broadcasts from our studio. Harvey was a pilot and would frequently fly alone to different locations for personal appearances, making several of those appearances in Denver. I was the morning editor at KBTR and I was told to look through the morning news copy and prepare a stack of stories for Mr. Harvey to look through that he might use for his broadcast. Then he would head to the production studio and with the production manager (my friend Van Kyrious) they would record his next broadcast for national distribution.

One morning Harvey wasn't real impressed with the news stories we had. He started interviewing, not on the air, our young production director. At that time Van was in his 20s and had moved to Colorado from the East. When Paul Harvey recorded his program that day there was a lengthy segment during which Mr. Harvey delivered entirely off the top of his head a description of this young man who was working selling shoes in Cleveland yearning to see open spaces in the West.

Paul Harvey's original ad-libbed piece about this young Eastern shoe salesman leaving the city to begin life anew in the West, based on a 5 minute conversation he'd had moments before he hit the air, actually tugged at your heart strings. An amazing work from a true artist. It was to me an awesome demonstration of Paul Harvey's expertise and ability to create a human communication that touched every listener. Talk about extemporaneous and impromptu speaking demonstrations. He was skilled and brilliant. His penchant for dramatic pause was legendary.

Mr. Harvey, like me was a *radio baby* starting at the age of 14 at KVOO in his home town of Tulsa, Oklahoma. I'd worked at three radio stations in three different states, including my first station KYOU, that claimed to have been a place Paul Harvey had worked when he was young. He passed away on February 28, 2009 at the age of 90.

On the first day of our station visits the three of us arrived in Garden City, Kansas, which was the place of my birth, my father's birthplace and his father's birthplace. Our first stop was a radio station whose manager was a little plump and a lot grouchy. He obviously would be a tough sell. To break the ice I informed him my family was from Garden City. "Oh?" he responded with some interest. I said "yes, my Mother and Father actually met when both were Junior college students in Garden City". He asked "What was your Dad's name?" I said Robert Cooper. His face scrunched up and he growled "Yes I knew him he ran off and married my girl friend!" (My Mother). We didn't make any deals with him.

Our Nebraska Baby

One snow covered Scottsbluff day my wife presented me with our third child, a baby girl. We had decided to try to have a third child for we both had hoped for a girl and we had been blessed with two boys. It was as though someone upstairs was listening and I've frequently thought about the huge smile my little bride displayed when she learned the new baby was a girl. We had named our boys Troy and Travis, thinking those were good masculine western names. If it had been a boy the name was going to be "Trevor" but we hadn't really come up with a good name for a girl starting with "TR." We settled on "Trina" which would legally become "Katrina". As she grew older she became known by her friends as "Tina" and she is still called that today. What will be will be.

During my daughter's third year of life we decided to take our growing family on a driving trip to California. We would take our time and take the children to the Four Corners, see the Cliff Dwellings at Mesa Verde, Colorado, drive across what was then the World's highest independent suspension bridge, have a foot race on the Bonneville Salt Flats, see the Grand Canyon, return through Yellowstone Park, and somewhere between visit my mother in California and of course Disneyland.

Before leaving I did a little research about agriculture in California. It appeared to be an agricultural gold mine. Some 250 different commercial crops were grown in California. Agriculture was one of the leading industries in that state and there was no active farm radio network other than recorded programs circulated by the California Farm Bureau. When we returned from our family journey I convinced my partners we should be signing up stations in California. Our sales were made based on how many acres of what particular kind of crop was raised in the areas covered by stations carrying my programs. Initially we signed up a major broadcast station in Fresno, in Merced, and one in Sacramento.

For several months I phoned in my daily broadcasts to those California stations from Nebraska, and then decided to take the chance, move to California, sign up more stations and base our network out of the Fresno area instead of Nebraska. The partners agreed with some trepidation. We sold our home in Scottsbluff thinking we made enough on the sale to easily qualify to buy a home in California. We liked the city of Visalia, about 45 minutes from Fresno. When we arrived we couldn't find a home in Visalia we could afford. We thought about renting but the first rental we looked at was housing a number of live frogs in the living room and we spotted a couple of live snakes in the basement and needless to say made a hasty retreat.

I was also driving up and down the state trying to line up other radio stations to carry my broadcasts and I was still broadcasting live and direct via telephone to the stations in Colorado, Nebraska, Kansas and Wyoming. Although I'd been to California a number of times visiting my Mother I still had this Colorado-bred mental image of a land where the sun is always shining and in every back yard there's a pool by which young ladies in bikinis are always lounging. That bubble popped quickly. We finally found a house to rent. It was a ranch home located at the center of a raisin farm fertilized by extremely foul smelling chicken waste. The nearest town was a tiny berg called Fowler. It was about ten miles from Fresno. It was winter. It was cold. It was extremely foggy. So foggy each weekday morning we huddled around the TV set early in the morning to determine if the school buses were going to brave the fog and take our children to school. One month after we moved into this house we received a utility bill which totaled over $450 for electrical power alone. We had not been aware that this house was heated with water pipes located in the floor through which hot water was distributed; the water was heated in a huge water tank heated with electricity?

I did manage to sign up a total of about eight radio stations in California to carry our broadcasts but the folks in Nebraska were not happy about listening to farm broadcasts from somebody in California not Nebraska. Nebraska, Colorado, Kansas, Wyoming farmers never really considered California farmers their kind of people. In fact one old timer in Nebraska, when I told him I was headed for California suggested I was headed for the "Land of Fruits and Nuts" where the farmers wore thousand dollar suits and didn't even get to the office until 10 a.m. It is truly remarkable, when one thinks about it, the perceptions we all have of places we've never really seen except in movies and television sit-coms. To Nebraskans a woman marrying a California farmer was like Zsa Zsa Gabor living on the Farm called "Green Acres".

A few months after starting the California network, I received a letter from my partners saying the Nebraska broadcasts weren't working originating from California. My partners recommended they give me sole ownership of California and they would operate Nebraska, Colorado, Wyoming and Kansas. I did keep the California broadcasts going for more than 15 years, not significantly profiting but I kept producing.

Our national sales person asked if I would consider moving my network base to California's Imperial Valley because he represented a radio station there that needed an NAFB broadcaster on its staff. The station he was referring to was located in the cotton, wheat, melon and cattle country kept alive with Colorado River water in the desert near the Mexican border. Agriculture was everything in that area. The station owner was a very affable man who'd retired from a successful advertising agency career in San Diego and purchased this little radio station in the desert.

He wanted me to become his News Director, Farm Director, part-time DJ and would provide space and equipment for me to continue my broadcasts each day to the other stations (he also joined my network). The new headquarters for my California network (I changed the named from *Agribiznet* to *Agribusiness Today Radio Network*) was of all places Brawley, California. Driving to Brawley from the Fresno area was an eye-opening experience. You swear you are headed for the end of the Earth. The road narrows (or did at that time) to two lanes, you pass the largest body of polluted water in California. The Salton Sea was created many years ago by flooding of Colorado River Water.

We remained in Brawley for about three years (much to the chagrin of my wife). I grew to like the desert. You could turn on the cold water to take a shower during the summer and get hot water. Our neighbor's swimming pool was always heated. Although I didn't like selling advertising time I was given some accounts to handle across the border in Mexicali (no, I didn't speak much Spanish). The cotton growers held their regular meetings at our radio studio live on the air. The weekends saw an endless stream of vehicles pulling trailers loaded down with four-wheelers. Families were trying to escape Los Angeles and San Diego for a few days.

The busiest place for a hundred miles was the emergency room at the Brawley Hospital, mostly neck injuries occurring when young ATV drivers (some 4 and 5 years old) would accidentally drive off the top of a hill in the nearby desert sand dunes. Surprisingly the schools in Brawley were excellent. All three of my children were placed in a special "gifted program" and the schools were small enough that there was freedom for teachers to tap into their creativity. The winter days in Brawley saw perfect weather conditions with temperatures ranging from the low 70s to the low 80s.

The winter population would increase when "snow birds" from the North especially Canada, would park their campers on empty cement foundations in a remote section of the desert that once served as a military training center. During World War Two General George Patton selected the desert site near the tiny desert town of Niland for a training compound to prepare troops for the invasion of North Africa. In the 1960s the buildings at the site were removed but the concrete slabs beneath buildings remained. Since the government abandoned the site it has served as a permanent home for about 150 people with the population blooming to as many a 5-thousand during the winter months. It is called "Slab Town." "Slabbers" as they are referred to became some of my most consistant listeners. I would receive calls and notes from them frequently mentioning they enjoyed listening to my show when it begins at 4 oclock in the morning.

When I eventually moved to another station in Northern California I would still receive calls from people who had listened to my show in Slab Town and were glad I'd moved north. When I arrived at the station, as early as 3:30 AM to turn on the transmitter the control room would be occupied by three inch long cockroaches (I kid you not) Because afternoon temperatures there usually soared around 125 degrees Fahrenheit a lot of folks started very early to avoid the afternoon sun.

The Imperial Valley was a living laboratory for entomologists having nearly every species of living bugs imaginable. I named each of the roaches that greeted me and often would have conversations with them on the air (thinking at that time of day no one was listening anyway) but to my delight that drew several phone calls each day.

When my wife couldn't stand it anymore I would take her to San Diego, about 2 hours away for the weekend. At that time there were few places to shop in Brawley. I do remember there was a bar, located in a historic building in the downtown section (actually they were almost all historic) that made the best burgers I'd ever eaten (next to Harry's Drive-in of course back in Greeley.) Each of the three years I was working in Brawley I made the annual journey to Kansas City to try not to politic with our fellow farm broadcasters.

The Program Director was an attractive young lady who I would at times intentionally frustrate. I remember one morning I was finishing up my morning broadcast and I played Marie Osmond's old hit "Paper Roses." This young lady screamed out "My God Cooper!" When the

87

song ended I told my audience "There's an ole country hit from that pretty 'little bit country' girl Marie. I'm gonna close now with another country hit by guitarist Les Paul and his country classy wife Mary Ford" (I heard our young program director yell "Who???"). I'd end with an extemporaneous contest "the first person who can tell me how many footsteps you hear during this song wins a free pass to next week's rodeo now that's as country as you're going to get" the record by the way was called the "*Walkin' and Whistlin' Blues*." I honestly forget how many steps you could hear through the song but there was a winner. When I stepped out of the control room the young program director glared at me and said "We gotta Talk". I told her "Sorry, got a sales call to make in Mexicali" and I darted out the door. We never did have that talk.

The station owner was a railroad hobbyist and actually owned an antique sleeper car he maintained in Mexicali, Mexico. My family took a train ride one weekend to a small fishing village in Mexico. Jack was allowed to add his car to the train. It was a good deal of fun. The train was packed with folks from San Diego who boarded with large coolers filled with beer. By the time the train reached its destination, where we were to spend a couple of hours then return to Mexicali, the beer coolers were empty and were re-filled with fresh shrimp purchased from the shrimp boat fishermen in Mexico.

I was contacted by a radio station manager from Yuba City, California. He was interested in carrying my farm radio broadcasts. I made an appointment to drive to Yuba City (45 miles North of Sacramento quite a distance from our Mexican border town area) and promised if he signed up for my broadcasts I would stay in town a couple of extra days to help his sales people pitch sponsorship of the broadcasts. I did and while I was visiting he wanted to know if I'd be interested in becoming his News and Farm Director. He was changing to an all-news format and needed the expertise.

At one time Rand McNally issued a report ranking Yuba City, California as the worst place to live in the entire nation due to a lack of culture, museums etc. but those of us who lived there vigorously protested. Yuba City was in a major Northern California farming area (fruit orchards and rice). There was a large population of people of East Indian heritage who's ancestors had migrated there because growing conditions were identical to those of the Punjab area.

Most were farmers. In fact local Yuba City natives told stories of these folks visiting farm owners in the area carrying suitcases filled with cash offering to buy up farm properties. When a deal was reached the buyers would notify relatives back in India and inform them they could join them to farm in America. Many did. There is an annual parade in Yuba City which attracts thousands of the East Indian heritage from all over the United States to Yuba City.

I took my wife with me to Yuba City so she could see the community. The first comment she made was the area actually had trees and stores to shop in. That was enough for her. As it turned out my family ended up living in Yuba City for more than twenty years. We waited to actually move until my oldest son finished his Junior High School graduation in Brawley. He would be starting High School in Yuba City. We'd rented a U-Haul truck which was packed to the gills and as soon as the graduation ceremony ended in Brawley we were on the road. The truck was so full we left a small motor driven pick-up truck the children had won in a contest. My oldest son had driven the little truck in the annual "Cattle Call" parade in Brawley. We left the little truck with a neighbor, fully intending to return someday to get it. We never have. I also left a very large cardboard box filled with recorded interviews on reel-to-reel tapes I'd done with more than 150 celebrities and about 40 radio documentary broadcasts I'd produced. They'd gotten mixed in with some old reel to reel tapes I'd inadvertently given to a neighbor who'd just purchased a stereo reel to reel tape deck and had no reels for it. That was indeed an idiotic mistake and we've never retrieved those either. I didn't leave my heart in Brawley but I did leave everything else.

Although we remained in Yuba City for more than twenty years, I worked at KOBO for 6 of those years. Again I was the news director, farm director, and disc jockey whatever was needed. I co-hosted the morning show we called "Coffee and Conversation" and continued to produce and phone my farm network reports to several California stations four times a day. Listenership was good but the station's signal didn't carry much past the city limits and there were two other radio stations in town providing stiff competition. With my children all settling into school we were reluctant to move again.

I took a supplemental job teaching a class in broadcasting for adults and students from three area high schools for three hours every afternoon. It was a task I agreed to for three years. We had a small broadcast station set up at Marysville, California High School, across the river from Yuba City. The audio programming was broadcast on the local cable television system.

One of my students in that class for all 3 years was a young man named Eric Houston. Eric was a student at Lindhurst High School in near-by Olivehurst. Students from Lindhurst and Yuba City High Schools were bussed each day to Marysville High School for my broadcasting class. Eric, angered at his Civics teacher for giving him a failing grade and blocking his participation in graduation exercises walked into his high School on May 1, 1992 carrying a 12 gauge pump action shotgun and a sawed off .22 caliber rifle, wearing a vest packed with ammunition. He walked directly into the teacher's classroom and shot and killed him. The teacher's name was Robert Brens. Houston expressed frustration in addressing other students at the school that he'd been just one point below failing and Bren refused to give him another chance. Houston had rented a tuxedo and a limo to attend the graduation dance and had lost his job. Eric also shot and killed 17 year old Judy Davis while in Mr. Bren's classroom. He then walked into the hallway and shot and killed another student, Jason Edward White. He pointed a gun at another female student but before he fired, a student named Beamon Hill pushed the girl out of the way and Beaman was shot in the side of his head. Houston then entered another classroom where he held 30 students and the teacher hostage. He ordered one of the students to get more students and bring them into the classroom. Another 50 students were added to those being held at gunpoint.

Houston held off police for a full 8 hours and finally surrendered. By then 9 others had been wounded. Houston was later convicted and sentenced to death. The last I heard he was being held at San Quentin awaiting an execution date. He was a very quiet student and seemed very shy in my class. Despite his shyness and reluctance to go on the air he returned each year. The gravity and reality of the tragedy is not something you would forget and there is no logic. The impact on other students, teachers and the families of all involved simply can't be adequately expressed in words. In 1997 a movie based on the incident was released, starring Freddie Prinze Jr. and Henry Winkler entitled *The Siege of Johnson High* also known as *Hostage High* or *Target for Rage*.

I took on a variety of odd jobs to help pay the bills. I also managed to purchase turntables, amplifier, mixer board, microphones and speakers to enable me to make extra money as a mobile DJ for parties and weddings. In addition, about this same time I was hired by a local businessman, whose wife was counting on inheriting some money and he wanted, at the urging of another man that I'll kindly refer to as an entrepreneur, to start a communication company. The first project would be a local daily business newsletter. I would write the stories in the evening, then deliver the finished copies to a local printer and the next evening we would pick up the copies and distribute them throughout the two cities, Yuba City and Marysville. We called this publication "TC Business News" (TC = Twin Cities). I also covered radio shifts on Saturdays and Sundays on a radio station in Chico (about 40 miles north of Yuba City) to make extra money. That lasted 4 years. The radio class lasted 3 years, the DJ gigs lasted 25 years and the Business News venture lasted 6 months.

Meantime back at KOBO,

The owner decided it was time to move on and sell his broadcast license and radio station lock, stock and barrel. The buyer was a local dermatologist who grew up listening to KGO in San Francisco. He jumped in with both feet. He hired a great manager who'd been the News Director for all-news KFWB in Los Angeles and other similar properties. I remained news anchor, talk show host, and even hosted a program where folks would call-in items they wanted to sell or buy (we called it "Radio Tradio").

The station sounded better than ever before. We'd expanded the staff, improved our radio signal, adopted the Los Angeles All-news station KFWB's fast moving news format and felt we were doing well. We sounded like a big city operation. But the fact was, even though it was better, the station still didn't have much transmitter power and our sales people were trying to charge higher rates in a community with no real economic base other than farming. It was also only 45 miles from Sacramento where radio stations delivered tough competition with multiple all-news all-talk formats.

One December day the new owner's financial advisers recommended he shut down the station. The station was silent for the first time in 50 years. The shutdown drew the attention of the Sacramento Bee and local newspapers. A front page story with my picture detailing the downfall of our station appeared in the Sacramento Bee the next day. The station was later auctioned off. The buyer was a company in San Francisco that broadcast primarily foreign language programming from San Francisco. The old KOBO simply re-broadcast those programs.

I did some work for the other radio station in Yuba City, and even traded anchoring their news and doing a DJ shift for advertising my mobile DJ service, including a booth at a Bridal Fair the station sponsored and a book listing pending weddings. That worked well but before I could fulfill my commitment to do the dances (my son Troy ended up doing most of them) I was contacted to interview for a new job.

The Interviews

Looking back over the 36 years I devoted to broadcasting I believe one of the greatest benefits was the access the jobs provided to interesting, creative and even famous people. I was gifted with opportunities to work with extremely talented and intelligent co-workers and to make acquaintances and conversations with a wide variety of celebrities, political leaders and historical leaders. Before I switch gears to review the Government career I thought I should share with you some of the people I was allowed to interview. Each truly having a place in shaping and molding our society.

Me and Pearl Buck

Author Pearl Buck

When I interviewed Pearl Buck she was working to collect donations for homeless children throughout the world. She was an author and a missionary. Her book *The Good Earth* was the best selling fiction novel in 1939. She was awarded a Pulitzer Prize and was the first woman to receive the Nobel Prize for literature. Her parents were missionaries in China. She wrote as many as 50 books. Our discussion focused on work being done at the time by the Pearl Buck Foundation to help children with developmental disorders. She passed away, a few years after this interview in 1973 at the age of 83.

Former FCC Commissioner Nicholas Johnson

Nicholas Johnson was best known for his sharp criticism of television news and entertainment. He was the one dissenting opinion among the Federal Communications Commission on which he sat from 1966 to 1973. Johnson originated the oft-quoted description of television as a "vast Wasteland".

Before we went on the air for my interview with him he talked in detail about what he felt was lacking in TV newscasts. He later wrote me a letter admitting he found my news broadcasts "stimulating and appropriate" and said he'd enjoyed our on-air discussion.

Pool Shark Minnesota Fats

His real name was Rudolph Wonderone Jr. from the Bronx. Until the movie "Hustler" was released in 1961 he was better known as "New York Fats". The film was a fictional biography in which he was portrayed by Jackie Gleason. In the film Minnesota Fats is challenged by a young pool hustler played by Paul Newman.

Wonderone told me the film was so popular he actually changed his name to the movie's character "Minnesota Fats". I interviewed him and his wife at their suite at Denver's Brown Palace as "Fats" downed a large platter containing about a dozen large sweet rolls in one setting.

He was a pleasant man who loved to laugh and he related funny stories about the trouble he and his best friend "Augie" had gotten into while growing up in Brooklyn. In 1971 he played himself in the movie "Player". Unfortunately he has passed on.

Film Producer-Director Stanley Kramer

Stanley Kramer was often considered to be the first "message movie" producer. His films include *The Defiant One, On the Beach, Judgment at Nuremberg, It's a Mad Mad Mad World, Ship of Fools, Guess Who's Coming to Dinner and Inherit the Wind*. We discussed what he liked to do at home with his family and not surprisingly he said the evening meals at his home with his wife and children usually became family forums for political and current affairs debates. His family, he said, loved to discuss, cuss and debate. He passed away in 2001 at the age of 87 at his choice for retirement, Bellevue, Washington.

Radio-TV Host Art Linkletter

Art Linkletter's real name was Gordon Arthur Kennedy. He was born in Moosejaw, Canada but was abandoned by his birth parents when he was 4 weeks old. He was adopted by an Evangelical Preacher and his wife and grew up in San Diego where he started his broadcast career as an announcer at KGB. He was best known for hosting the long running radio and television program "People are Funny" and later "Kids say the Darnest Things". He and his wife Lois Forrester were married for 75 years. They had five children outliving three of them. My interview with him focused on the death of his 20 year old daughter. In 1969 she committed suicide by jumping out of a 6th floor kitchen window. She was a student at UCLA at the time and he blamed her death on a "Flashback" from LSD use. Her death sparked a lifelong anti-drug use campaign by Mr. Linkletter. He passed away at the age of 97 in 2010 in Los Angeles.

Pianist Liberace

From the early 1950s through the mid-70s Liberace was the highest paid entertainer in the World. I found him to be very approachable, very friendly and easy to interview because he was actually very unassuming. He was born and raised in a suburb of Milwaukee. He was of Polish and Italian descent. He was a twin but his twin brother died at birth. His father was a laborer and factory worker who played the French Horn and loved music. His mother didn't care that much about music and was angered when his father paid for piano lessons for him when he was 4 years old. It turned out he was a child prodigy and a musical genius.

During my interview with him I referred to his "concert" to which he replied "I don't give concerts, I put on a show," truer words were never spoken. For one series of Las Vegas performances he actually featured "The Dancing Waters" that my Mother worked with on stage with him. He wore extravagant clothing and jewelry and featured a variety of sparkly and unusual pianos.

I clearly remember in the early 50s my Grandmother never missing his weekly television broadcast. He would often respond to harsh critics by saying "Yes, I cryed all the way to the bank." His real name was Wladzin Valentino Liberace. He passed away at his Palm Springs home in 1987 at the age of 67.

Actor Gig Young

Gig Young told me during an interview that I broadcast with him in Denver in 1970 that he was often referred to as "the other guy" because of the number of films in which he was cast in "other guy" roles through the 50s. His real name was Byron Barr. He grew up in Washington D.C. In 1940 he was cast in a movie playing a character named "Gig Young". Because at the time there was another film actor named Byron Barr, the studio asked him to change his performance name to "Gig Young" permanently. From 1940 to 1978 he appeared in many film and television roles. He won an Academy Award for his role in the 1969 movie "They Shoot Horses Don't They?" He was plagued during his later years with alcohol addiction. On October 19, 1978, three weeks after marrying 21 year old German actress Kim Schmidt, the couple's bodies were found in their Manhattan apartment.

Police said it appeared Gig Young had shot and killed his fifth wife, then shot and killed himself.

Actor Lee Marvin

When I met Lee Marvin he was in a Denver theater lobby handing out comment cards for people who'd just viewed one of his films (*Monte Walsh*). Marvin was the son of a New York advertising executive. His mother was a fashion writer and a beauty consultant. He'd joined the Marine Corps during World War II and was wounded during the "Battle of Saipan". When he returned to the mainland and took up acting he was cast for a number of 1950s films playing a soldier. In 1965 he won an Academy Award for his role in the film *Cat Ballou*. By the late 1960s Marvin had played a wide variety of roles and was becoming very popular. In fact he was making a million dollars per film. Following a series of illnesses Lee Marvin died of a heart attack in 1987.

Actor Roger Moore

Roger Moore's dad was a policeman and his mother was a housewife in Stockwell, England. He was an only child. When he turned 18 he joined the Royal Army Service Corps, achieved the rank of Captain and supervised a post in Germany. He transferred to the military's entertainment service and took acting lessons for a limited time at the Royal Academy of Dramatic Art.

Moore visited our television studios in Denver to promote a new television series in which he and Tony Curtis starred called *"The Persuaders"*. The series wasn't very successful but soon after, Moore took on the role of James Bond, a part he played for 12 years. For our interview Moore joined me at a conference room table, offered me a cigar (which I declined) lit up a huge cigar, puffed big clouds of smoke in my face—and then said "If you're ready I'm ready."

He was really entertaining. "Tell me Mr. Moore," I said "how does a guy from Wales like you go from a small town in England to become an International Movie Star?" "Well Larry," he responded laughingly, "Tell me how does a guy from Greeley, Colorado end up asking an International Movie Star like me how he came to be a movie star?'

Actress Jacqueline Bisset

I interviewed the beautiful Jacqueline Bissett during the filming of a movie entitled *"Stand Up and Be Counted"* in Denver. The film, which was directed by former child star Jackie Cooper, was not a very big hit and many years later I was reading an interview that Jacqueline Bissett had done with an entertainment writer in which she expressed frustration at movies targeting teens that really offered an actress nothing to give. She said "the camera just kind of brushes by you and you are unable to give anything". Be that as it may Jacqueline Bisset has performed in many films through the years that have provided her the opportunity to give the

97

audience thought provoking and expert characterizations and emotions. She has had a remarkable career.

Actress. Writer, Producer Lee Purcell

I met Lee Purcell on the set of *Stand and be Counted* in Denver in 1972. I was told if I would accompany her to her dressing trailer I could interview her as she prepared for her next scene. I told her I'd read that several critics were comparing her work to Actress Jane Fonda—their voice and speech patterns were somewhat the same. She said that was a compliment.

Lee Purcell was actually born at the Marine Corps Station Cherry Point in North Carolina. She is now (2011) 64 and she has enjoyed a long and fairly successful career. Growing up, as with most military families she moved frequently, finally settling in Arkansas. She attended college in Missouri majoring in acting and dance. In 1967 she moved to Los Angeles and supported herself with modeling jobs and television commercials. Two years later she was selected from 500 others auditioning for a part in a movie starring Steve McQueen entitled *Adam at Six A.M.* During the early 70s she moved to England to study acting at the Royal Academy of Dramatic Arts. That was at the conclusion of filming the movie in Denver. Several television and movie roles followed when she returned to Los Angeles in 1978. To prepare for the role of a 16 year old high school student in a film entitled *Almost Summer,* she actually enrolled as a student at North Hollywood High School. She said the principal and the teachers knew she was an actress but fellow students did not.

At one time she actually owned a video production company. She has been married three times and has a son who is also an actor, Dylan. She is a pilot, a competitive shooter, appears in rodeos and is a former Director of the National Rifle Association.

Actor Gary Lockwood

Gary Lockwood was a former College football star and stuntman who also had a healthy career as an actor. He was once married to actress Stephanie Powers. He is now (2011) 74 and married to Denise DuBarry. He starred in a long list of television series and films. His best known role was that of Dr. Frank Poole in *2001 A Space Odyssey*. For our interview he talked about how he virtually starved when he left the University of California to pursue an acting career. He said that was the most humbling experience of his life. He also discussed how demanding and unusual his role in *2001 A Space Odyssey* really was. He said it was an intense and physically demanding challenge that he would never forget.

Actress Edie Adams

Edith Elizabeth Eakee from Kingston, Pennsylvania grew up to become a glamorous television and Broadway personality. Her stage name was Edie Adams. As a child her mother taught her to sing and play the piano, they both appeared regularly in church. Her Grandmother taught her to sew. In fact from the 6th grade on Edie made her own clothing and started a designer clothing line and later her own cosmetics and beauty product companies. She graduated from the Julliard School of Music and the Columbia School of Drama. She studied at the Actors Studio in New York City. She couldn't decide at one point whether to pursue a career as an entertainer or as a designer. She tossed a coin and the entertainer won.

She appeared on the Milton Berle Television show, Arthur Godfrey's Talent Scouts and regularly on comedian Ernie Kovacs television show. In 1954 she married Kovacs. Just 8 years later Kovacs was killed in a car accident.

She made appearances on television and Broadway and for several years was the pitch person for Muriel Cigars. One

of Kovacs trademarks was chewing on a cigar. She passed
away in 2008 of cancer and pneumonia.

TV Host Dick Cavett and wife, Carrie Nye

One day, while working at Channel Nine in Denver I
was approached by an out-of-breath Assistant Manager who
told me I had to quickly grab a portable tape recorder and
jump into the back seat of a Limousine parked in front of the
television studios. He said the occupants were on their way
to the Airport but agreed to let me ride with them and record
our conversation for my radio show. He neglected to tell me
who I would be interviewing.

When I opened the back door, Dick Cavett and his
wife Carrie Nye were graciously waiting for me, introduced
themselves, I turned on my recorder and the conversations
just flowed. It was as though we had known one another for
many years. They had been back to Cavett's home territory
in Nebraska visiting and had to return to Los Angeles. Cavett
was very "Nebraska". Just the way he was on television, soft
spoken, obviously a careful listener and was logically reactive.
His wife had the persona of a glamorous actress, wonderful
long blond hair, perfectly groomed with an eloquent manner
of speaking with a deep voice that spoke "dramatic movie
star."

The two met one another when both were attending Yale
University. They were married in 1964 in New York City and
although they admittedly had a turbulent relationship, they
remained together until Carrie passed away in 2006. Cavett
remarried in 2010 in New Orleans.

TV Writer Producer David Victor

When he was a young man, Russian-born David Victor
wanted to be a doctor. He told me that due to the depression
in the 1930s he and his widowed mother experienced some

very difficult times just surviving. David Victor became a writer, a teller of stories and eventually a producer.

He was 13 when he and his widowed mother came to America from Odessa, Russia. As a young man Victor wrote scripts for radio dramas and the Mel Blanc Comedy Show. When television started to get legs he switched to writing stories for television. He was the writer and Associate Producer of *The Rebel, Trooper Hook*, and he wrote episodes of *Daniel Boone, Rawhide* and *The Texan*. David Victor produced *The Man from UNCLE, The Girl from UNCLE, Lucas Tanner, Owen Marshall, Counselor at Law Women, Vanished* and others. He produced *Dr. Kildare* and he wrote and produced one of the highest rated television series in history, *Marcus Welby, M.D.* That show aired for eight years starring Robert Young.

David Victor had a talent for bringing words to life and providing dialogue viewers found believable and compelling. Unfortunately David Victor suffered a fatal heart attack in 1989 while vacationing in Williamsburg, Virginia.

Actor-Director Jackie Cooper

Jackie Cooper was a child actor, an adult actor, a producer, a director and a film executive. His real name is John Cooper. His mother was also a former child star. His biological father left when Jackie was 2 years old. His Grandmother frequently worked as a movie extra and took the child with her for extra auditions. When Jackie was 3 he was cast in his first movie that was in 1926. He was known, in the earliest films as "Leonard".

Two more roles were offered him in 1929. The director of those two films recommended the child audition for the *Our Gang* comedy series produced by Hal Roach. Jackie was signed to a three year contract. In the spring of 1931 Jackie was loaned to Paramount Studios to appear in a film entitled *Skippy* for which Jackie was nominated for an Academy Award for Best Actor. He was only 9 years old and the youngest actor ever to be nominated for Best Actor.

In 1989 Cooper retired from the film industry and spent a good deal of his time training and racing horses at Hollywood Park and during the Del Mar racing season near San Diego. I found Jackie Cooper to be approachable, interesting to talk with and very open in his question responses. I think he's an under-respected Hollywood legend. Jackie Cooper passed away in May, 2011, he was 88.

Comedian George Gobel

George Gobel was best known for his own television program *The George Gobel Show.* He started his career as a country music singer on a program called *National Barn Dance* on WLS radio in Chicago, Gobel's Hometown. He too had an impressive military career serving as a flight instructor for the Army Air Corps during World War II, stationed in Oklahoma where he taught pilots to fly the B-26 Marauder bombers and the AT-9 Aircraft. When he was discharged at the end of the war he switched from singing to comedy.

He was low key, very understated and very funny. His routine involved past experiences and stories and sketches about "Alice" based on his real wife who he'd refer to as "Spooky Ole Alice." He labeled himself "Ole Lonesome George" and he coined phrases that became trendy including "I'll be a dirty bird"—"You don't hardly get those any more" and others. George Gobel passed away in 1991 after undergoing heart surgery.

Comedian Red Skelton

I met Red Skelton unexpectedly one day around 1965 in Casper, Wyoming. Skelton's second wife, Georgia Maurine Davis grew up in Casper, graduating from Natrona County High School. Skelton accompanied his wife for a tour of

Casper, visiting locations she remembered including her former home. Skelton stopped at the television station to ask if someone might help guide the couple. Because I was the news director and had asked to record an interview with him (a request he initially denied) I was selected. He was very quiet during the tour until his camera jammed. He tapped me on the shoulder and asked if I knew the location of a good camera store. I guided them to a store downtown. He walked into the store and asked the somewhat startled clerk to provide him the most reliable camera in the shop, a supply of film and batteries and a good flash. He made the purchase and we continued.

A couple of hours after I returned to my office Mr. Skelton unexpectedly returned to the studio, asked for me and said now he was ready to do an interview.

He and Georgia were married in 1945 and they had two children, Richard Jr. and Valentina Marie Skelton. When Richard was 10 years old, May 10, 1958 Richard died of Leukemia. Skelton was devastated. In 1966 Georgia wounded herself in what appeared to be an accidental shooting but she survived.

In 1971 Red and Georgia divorced. On the 10th anniversary of the death of their son Georgia committed suicide by gunshot. She was 55 years old. For the next decade Skelton refused to perform. He focused on his art. He specialized in paintings of clowns. Some of his paintings have sold for as much as $100,000 dollars each. He died in September of 1997 of pneumonia at his home at Rancho Mirage, California. He was 84 years old. Red Skelton had an incredible career. The characters he created for his performances will always be remembered. He was a comic genius the stuff of which legends are made.

Singer Patti Page

Nice is the term that comes to my mind when thinking about my interview with Patti Page. I recorded an interview with her in the early 60s, a period when many of the traditional singing stars of the 50s were losing popularity to rock and roll. Patti Page managed to continue to sell records into the 70s, not an easy accomplishment. She was an extremely nice person. She's had a long and successful career. Her records sold more than 100 million copies. She was the best-selling female artist for the entire decade of the 50s. Her first recordings were released in 1947. In 1950 she had her first number one million seller "*With my eyes Wide Open, I'm Dreaming*". Between 1950 and 1965 she had fourteen more million selling singles including one that stayed on the top of the charts for 5 months "*How Much is that Doggie in the Window*". My favorite young reality check girl Elizabeth knew about that song.

Actor Denver Pyle

Denver Pyle was a natural and in many ways resembled some of the great characters he played like Uncle Jesse in *The Dukes of Hazard*, Mad jack in *The Life and Times of Grizzly Adams*, Buck Webb, Doris Day's Father on *The Doris Day Show* and many others. His list of movie and television credits is long. My wife and I attended a party held for the participants of a film produced by Chares Pearce and filmed around Kalispell, Montana. Pyle was one of those rare people you meet and instantly get the feeling you've been friends with that person for years.

In 1994 he played opposite James Garner, Jodie Foster and Mel Gibson portraying a cheating card player who jumps off a riverboat to keep his dignity rather than be thrown off. His last role was reprising Jesse Duke in the 1997 film *The Dukes of Hazard: Reunion!* Denver Pyle died on Christmas Day, 1997 of lung cancer.

Actress Dawn Wells

Pat and I also met Dawn Wells at that Kalispell, Montana party for the cast and crew of the 1977 film *Winterhawk*. Dawn was raised in Reno and in 1959 was crowned Miss Nevada. She graduated from the University of Washington in Seattle with a degree in theater arts. Upon graduation she moved to Hollywood and landed minor roles in *77 Sunset Strip, Maverick,* and *Bonanza*. From 1964 until 1967 she played Mary Ann Summers on *Gilligan's Island*

Actress Karen Valentine

Karen Valentine is best known for her role as an idealistic young school teacher, "Alice Johnson" in the 1969 television series *Room 222*. I first met her one evening when I was scheduled to interview her for a radio broadcast in Denver. I remember it was dark as I was waiting at the front door of the broadcast studios to unlock the door for her when she arrived. When she came up to the front door, I opened it for her and she "floated in" wearing a large flowery hat and a very low cut silk flowing dress. Her husband at the time was Carl McLaughlin who arrived a few minutes later. Karen literally made an "entrance" for me as would a bonafide "star" and at that time she was. She was raised on a chicken farm in Northern California and had represented California in the "Miss Teenage America Pageant". She was also Miss Sonoma County and made the top 10 at the Miss California finals. She played "Gidget" in the film *Gidget Grows Up*, and in a short-lived television series in 1975 called *Karen* and appeared in several television programs and made for television movies. She and her husband got into some interesting almost heated exchanges during our broadcast—both were fun and excellent guests. They divorced in 1973 and she remarried songwriter Gary Verna in 1977.

Singer Patrice Munsel

Patrice Munsel loves Opera but when I interviewed her in the early 70s she talked about diversity. She'd appeared on many television programs and in musical theater. She was born in Spokane, Washington but studied singing and opera in New York. She was the youngest singer to star in the Metropolitan Opera, debuting when she was 18. She was nicknamed "Princess Pat". In 1943, her first role was the role of Philine in the Opera *Mignon*. In 1952 Munsel married New York Advertising Executive Robert Schuler. They were married for fifty-five years and had four children together. Schuler passed away in 2005. In 1958 Patrice ended her career as an opera singer and has since performed in many musical comedies.

Performer Carol Channing

Carol Channing was putting on a one woman show in Denver at the time I got an opportunity to interview her. I was told if I stood at a certain location in the theater she would walk right by and she might consent to an interview. She did walk by, I asked her politely if I could record a short radio interview with her for KBTR—She looked at me and pointed to an older man walking directly behind and said "ask him." He was her husband and manager at the time, Charles Lowe. He listened to my proposal and said loudly "Carol its O.K. come on back." She returned and we chatted for about 15 minutes. It was as though an "on" button was flicked. She was warm, friendly and funny.

When I closed the interview and thanked her she immediately picked up the same fast walking pace and moved on. She was born in Seattle, was into debate and extemporaneous speaking in high school and she was a practitioner of Christian Science. Her father was the Editor of the San Francisco Star when she was a child. She won three Tony Awards on Broadway, A Golden Globe and was nominated for an Academy Award. She drew national attention when she starred in Broadway's *Hello Dolly*. During the Broadway run she never missed a performance.

She's been featured in many movies and television shows and even does voice over work. She was the voice of Grandmamma Adams in the animated version of *The Adams Family*. She's been married four times. She was married to Mr. Lowe for 42 years but in 1998 she abruptly filed for divorce. He passed away before the divorce was final.

Actor Jesse White (The Maytag Man)

I met Jesse White when he appeared at the Central City Theater in Colorado working with Actor Gig Young in a stage version of *Harvey*. His real name was Jesse Marc Weidenfeld from Buffalo, New York. Although his film credits are long, he is best remembered as the Maytag repairman in television commercials, a role he played from 1967 to 1988. In the 1930s he worked a variety of jobs including lingerie salesman, vaudeville and burlesque performer and in 1942 he debuted on Broadway appearing in *The Moon is Down* and in the original Broadway version of *Harvey*. His last onscreen role was in an episode of *Seinfeld* in 1996. He and his wife, Celia Cohn had two daughters. His wife passed away in 2003. He died on January 9, 1997 from a heart attack following surgery just 5 days after his 80th birthday.

Me and Rush Limbaugh

Rush Limbaugh

I wasn't sure whether to list Rush as an entertainer or a political figure. I was familiar with his early work as a disc jockey in Missouri. When he was working as a talk show host in Sacramento I thought he was intentionally making ultra conservative rants to stir the pot. If that's true he's managed to take it to the extreme.

I talked with him one day when he was in Yuba City, Califormia promoting an appliance store that helped sponsor his show in Sacramento. Rush Limbaugh is another "Radio Baby" starting his radio career when he was 16. His first talk radio show was in 1984 at KFBK in Sacramento.

His family was active in Republican politics. In 1988 he was selected to host a national conservative broadcast originating at WABC in New York City. In 2008 he signed an 8 year $400 million extension contract that pays him $50 million per year. I'd always suspected his talk show began as a satire of pompous right wing conservatives but conservative America believed him and now I think he did too.

Jerry Clower—Comedian

Jerry Clower

For my morning show down in the California Desert I featured one of Jerry's great routines each morning and he would regularly call me and we'd joke live on the air. Jerry was a very religious and kind man who was blessed with a gift of humor. Jerry used stories about his friends and relatives in Mississippi and Louisiana to help sell fertilizer.

His stories became so popular his clients urged him to record some of his presentations. Jerry did that and sent some of the recordings to an acquaintance of mine, Big Ed Wilkes from Lubbock, Texas, a Farm Broadcaster. Big Ed contacted a record producer, MCA offered Clower a contract. He recorded several very popular records of his stories that brought in millions of dollars. For 27 years Jerry entertained folks and released 27 full recordings.

He was a member of the Grand Ole Opry and frequently hosted the *Country Crossroads* broadcasts. He passed away after heart surgery in August of 1998.

Richard and Karen Carpenter

The day I met the Carpenters I was to interview them at the Denver Air Terminal. I met Karen first. She was wearing a red sweatshirt and blue jeans. She was disarmingly normal despite the fact the Carpenters recordings had set sale records World wide. When her brother Richard joined us they told me I should really be interviewing singer Mac Davis who'd been flying with them because his records were really taking off. I did interview Mac but after I'd completed my recording with the Carpenters. Karen and Richard were truly down to Earth talking openly about their childhood, how they thought they became so famous, singing warm ballads and "easy listening" arrangements in a rock and roll world.

Karen said she just wanted to play drums but one day when asked to sing, she did. She said she'd never had voice lessons or even thought about being a singer. She said "it just came out of nowhere". I discussed Christmas with them, a subject they each enjoyed discussing even though it was Summer when this interview was recorded. They discussed songs on their family's favorite Christmas album by, of all artists, Spike Jones. They hummed songs from that album, Karen singing a few bars and excitedly telling her brother "you know, the one!—Oh what was the name of that song?" I actually looked for and purchased that Spike Jones Christmas album and was surprised at the variety of straight choral arrangements featured in addition to the usual novelty fare. A few years later, when the Carpenters own Christmas albums (there were two) were released nearly every song was taken from that Spike Jones album. I like to think my unexpected discussion about Christmas with the Carpenters may have played a role in the release of those two great holiday discs.

Karen's death was tragic and I often think about that. Karen was an honest sweet girl who never thought she was a very good singer. She fought a losing battle with eating disorders that eventually caused the heart attack that killed her in February, 1983 at her parent's home at Downey, California. Karen's short marriage had failed, she was weak and depressed and she died on the same day she was scheduled to sign the divorce papers. Karen was a drummer—she loved playing drums but she sang like an angel and we miss her.

I also interviewed the following political leaders and news broadcasters:

President John F. Kennedy

I, as do many of us who were alive then still have a clear memory of the day President Kennedy was shot. I was preparing for a newscast and was leaning over a teletype machine. It was the only time in my career I ever saw the word "Flash" with 8 bells on a teletype—"President John F. Kennedy has been shot." I, like many of us will never forget that day.

Attorney General Robert Kennedy

The night Robert Kennedy was shot I was staying with the National Press Corps at a downtown hotel in Colorado Springs, Colorado. Vice President Hubert Humphrey was to deliver the commencement address for the graduating class at the U.S. Air Force Academy the next morning. The activity in that hotel when the television networks provided live coverage was immediate and frantic.

President Lyndon Johnson
Vice President and Mrs. Hubert Humphrey (Three Times)
President Richard Nixon (Three times)

While covering the Colorado Republican delegation at the National Republican Convention in Miami I saw first hand the pressure Nixon could impose to "convince" all members of the delegation to support his candidacy. In later years, underscored by his effort to cover-up the break-in at the Democratic Campaign headquarters at the Watergate Hotel what I'd suspected about Nixon appeared to be justified.

President Jimmy Carter
President Ronald Reagan (Three times)
Senator Frank Church (five times)
Senator George Romney
Senator Eugene McCarthy
Senator Barry Goldwater
Senator Mike Mansfield
News Correspondent Harry Reasoner
CBS News Correspondent Charles Kuralt

Chapter Five

Bugs Birds Cows
and Public Relations

I had submitted an application for a position as an information officer, should one open up with the State of California. It was April of 1990 and California Department of Food and Agriculture (CDFA), in a joint project with the United States Department of Agriculture's (USDA) Animal and Plant Health Inspection Service (APHIS) was involved in a multi-million dollar effort to eliminate an infestation of Mediterranean Fruit Flies from the entire Los Angeles Basin. The tiny flies had the ability to destroy a multitude of California crops.

These costly pests, who laid their eggs inside many exotic fruits and vegetables, had been transported into the Los Angeles area either by travelers from infested countries or black market style, smuggled in with and hidden beneath shipments of other legal products. The only known treatment at that time was the use of a chemical called Malathion. The Malathion was mixed with what amounted to a syrupy concoction intended to attract the flies so they would eat the Malathion and die off. To apply this mixture, a group of helicopters with spray attachments would fly very low in military formation, usually beginning after midnight over the entire Los Angeles Basin. At that time CDFA's Plant Industry Division employed one Information Officer. APHIS had provided four of its Public Affairs specialists but the story was getting attention from media throughout the U.S. and the World.

It was the top story in media-clogged Los Angeles. These five Information officers were fielding up to seventy reporter calls each day. I was hired as a limited term employee for three months. I would be living during that time at a motel near the project site in Los Angeles. I was interviewed for the job by the Director of the CDFA Plant Division, Dr. Isi Siddiqui (who later became the chief agricultural negotiator for the Obama Administration's U.S. Trade Representative.). I was to fly to Los Angeles the next day and I was handed a two-inch thick stack of documents containing everything you really never wanted to know about Fruit Flies.

The fly that devoured Los Angeles

The project site was on an old military base near El Monte, California. There was a collection of "trailer" type temporary buildings. To accept a job dealing with the Los Angeles news media is in itself a formidable challenge but I had no idea how challenging that would turn out to be. The first newspaper headline I saw on my arrival at my new job read like this "Malathion: Death from the Skies." Everything I'd read on the plane flying to LA indicated there was a very small amount (about 2 ounces for every acre sprayed—10% of a mixture that was 90% corn syrup) of Malathion (commonly used on flea collars and to spray neighborhoods for mosquitoes) yet the story described "squadrons of helicopters taking to the skies over Southern California spraying a deadly nerve agent originally developed by German scientists during World War II"(implying we are Nazi's?) This story continued "Now quietly and without fanfare, the United States Government has taken the first halting steps in a plan that could expand this poison project nationwide"

The newspaper reported there was evidence that the spray increased birth miscarriages and caused intrauterine growth retardation. The story claimed that 43 per cent of the families attending and participating in a little league baseball tournament that was sprayed suddenly became "deathly ill". That of course was never substantiated. It was definitely a hostile media in Los Angeles that fed like piranhas on every negative element even when 95% of the claims were proven to be completely exaggerated or simply untrue (after all, the story's the gold, accuracy wasn't all that important).

It was the first time I'd been placed in a position of defense. As a reporter you want to aggressively seek out issues, as a public affairs person for the Government you are immediately placed in a defensive posture. The trick is to learn to provide direct positive answers to questions, learn what not-to-say first and foremost, and still manage to develop a relationship of trust and believability with the media—phew!

By 1990 I had been behind the microphone for more than thirty years. To sit across the table from that microphone answering questions and not asking them was the toughest challenge of my career. My three month stint was renewed three times meaning I fought for the glory of Medfly spraying for a full nine months in Los Angeles, then was offered a permanent job with CDFA in Sacramento when I returned home. It was a job I held for 14 more years. During those fun-filled nine months I delivered roughly fifty presentations to civic groups, senior citizens, schools, telephone and utility company employees, even the Hollywood Rotary Club about the safety and proper use of Malathion to eliminate the Mediterranean Fruit Fly.

I was scheduled to publicly debate the reporter for the Los Angeles Times who'd been covering the Medfly crisis since its inception (and often mysteriously knew what was happening at our Medfly project Base before we did). I was declared the winner before I said a word because at the last minute he backed out so my debate became my speech. It was before the Los Angeles Chapter of the Public Relations Society of America. I received a number of complimentary letters from the civic and business groups I addressed telling about Malathion spraying.

I produced, filmed, wrote and narrated four different videos on the Medfly crisis. One focused on the process of breeding male Medflies in Hawaii and Mexico, irradiating the males making them sterile and dying them a bold red color so that when caught in the many traps around Los Angeles they could be easily identified as sterile males. The sterile flies were then shipped by the millions (after all they are fairly tiny) to our project in Los Angeles to be released by air and from the back of trucks. This was in the hope any wild females present would mate with the sterile males and produce no off-spring eventually disappearing.

Talk about strange scenes created by one's memory moments, I remember visiting a facility located in a warehouse section of Tijuana, Mexico where sterile flies were being prepared for releases at the U-S Mexico border. It brings to mind scenes from the fictitional television series about Counter Terrorist plots in "24." It was dark, there were two mysterious looking men watching the warehouse. We had to prove who we were and what we were doing there and then we all gathered around strange looking mesh containers filled with live flies. Unlike the television series, no bombs exploded and no machine gun fire was heard just the flapping of tiny wings.

When I first arrived for Medfly duty I learned my home would be an older Howard Johnson's Motel just off the Interstate. The first night I was awakened about 11 p.m. by the voices of angry men. I peeked through my bedroom window and saw about fifteen or twenty men gathered in a circle in the parking lot. I wasn't aware of it at the time but they were all scientists from my new employer, the California Department of Food and Agriculture who had been given what they considered to be lowly jobs. They were to carry bright flashlights and drive to assigned locations. Their task was to use the lights to help guide the squadron of helicopters stay on track.

Because of the volatile media coverage of our effort there was great concern about avoiding any "over spray" or "drifting" of the chemical. The applications had to be right on target and there could be no "wiggle room" so to speak. The Sacramento bosses reasoned because of the "delicacy" of the task, scientists would be the people to get it right. Scientists were not pleased and truly spent most of their time in the motel parking lot complaining to one another about their assignments.

I was required to attend a weekly meeting of a group of thirty medical doctors who were asked to evaluate complaints from residents and document any ill effects reported from the Malathion spray.

I flew along one night on one of the helicopters during one of their many flights. On this night they were spraying the Crystal Cathedral and Disneyland. The Crystal Cathedral is a church designed by famous architect Philip Johnson who used 10-thousand rectangular shaped panes of glass windows, not bolted on but glued with a silicone glue substance. The 26-hundred seat cathedral was the scene for Reverend Robert Schuler's weekly nationally televised services.

There was a good deal of concern about the spray mixtures adherence to all that glass. However the substance usually washed off easily with just water. It did leave a sticky coating and it did stick to the paint on cars but could be easily washed off. If not washed off, because the mixture contained protein, it could damage the paint, much as a raw egg would damage paint if not quickly rinsed off. I and a Federal information officer flew along that night for fear there might be protests or media interference at the airports. There was a lot of media interest about the daring effort to spray over Disneyland and the Crystal Cathedral. However there were no protestors and there surprisingly were no reporters or media helicopters monitoring our activities. One of the pilots did find a bullet hole in the back of the aircraft when we landed that night.

There were a ton of rumors and a lot of strange people popping up out of nowhere. An LA radio station scheduled a "harmonic convergence," suggesting everyone in Los Angeles go outside and march down the nearest street humming and/or playing kazoos with the theory this "harmonic convergence" would force the flies to flee. There was an organization calling themselves "the Breeders" that claimed to be breeding and releasing their own Medflies hoping to make the Medfly problem unmanageable and the spraying "financially intolerable." A group called the "Coalition against Urban Spraying" argued there was research proving that Malathion could cause cancer, perhaps but honestly folks "the poison is in the dose!"

There was also an outbreak of Mexican Fruit Fly in San Diego. Mexican fruit flies are a little larger than Medflies and don't have quite as many hosts but are still potentially economically disastrous. I was assigned to attend a protest demonstration there, outside a district courtroom where legal efforts were being made to try to stop aerial spraying. The scene was more colorful than a circus with media remote trucks lined up. Radio stations brought large brightly painted RV's. There were people dressed in gorilla suits and vendors wandering around peddling cotton candy.

It was during the period I worked at the Medfly Project I first met two men who would become "Cumpadres." Three months after I started working at the project the USDA hired a gentleman from Texas to join our Public Affairs team. His name was also Larry and he also came out of broadcasting. The other Federal public affairs staff started gradually returning to the Washington D.C. area, one by one until only "Larry and Larry" remained. We were often referred to as "Daryl and his other brother Daryl." That by the way from the old Bob Newhart Show.

That working relationship continued for many years. After Medfly, Larry was also hired fulltime by the USDA and eventually he too worked in Sacramento. The work we did was very similar and we were often in a joint Federal-State project situation.

Lalo Guerrero

The other person I met during this time period was a well known Hispanic entertainer, Lalo Guerrero. Shortly after returning to home base in Sacramento I was tasked with creating a public education program aimed at reducing the amounts of exotic fruits and vegetables being shipped or carried into California from foreign nations where Medflies were endemic. This required extensive efforts to reach Spanish speaking populations and Asian populations throughout California.

Another element of our campaign was the scheduling of meetings with business and community leaders for the many ethnic communities throughout California to raise awareness of the exotic fruit pest problem. We attended events at Buddhist Temples and hosted dinners during which I would talk, with a translator, about the problem—media would be invited and we'd usually get good coverage. We hosted dinners for the Thai communities, Laotian, Vietnamese, Chinese, Korean, Philippine and Spanish.

We contracted with Fleishman Hillard Public Relations in Los Angeles to help develop those campaigns. The Account Executive for our Spanish language outreach campaign recommended to me we locate a Hispanic entertainer to serve as a celebrity spokesman. She specifically recommended *Lalo Guerrero*. Lalo Guerrero was best known among the Latino populations for a series of thirty-three children's albums he'd recorded featuring three make-believe characters "Las Ardillitas," that translates to "Three Little Squirrels" who sounded much like the "Chipmunks". Lalo was well known for writing "Corridos," songs that told stories. He'd written a song used as an anthem during the battle for his friend Cesar Chavez and farm worker rights in California.

He also was praised by the Hispanic community for a song protesting the plight of Hispanic youth called "*No Chicanos on TV*". His biggest hit record was "*Poncho Lopez*", a parody of the TV show theme song "*The Ballad of Davy Crockett*". Lalo told me about getting a call from Walt Disney himself, who asked that Lalo come to Disney's Office for a talk about that record. Lalo said Disney was very polite and was concerned because technically Disney owned the rights to "Davy Crockett" and he felt there were some legal issues with Lalo's Poncho Lopez record (which by that time had sold thousands of copies) he said "I was a worried man" but he said he and Disney had a long talk, that they genuinely liked one another and Disney promised he wouldn't take any action against Lalo for the record. Lalo agreed never to sing the song during future performances and the two parted friends.

Lalo followed that success however with other parodies including "*Poncho Claus*" a parody of "*The Night Before Christmas*", and "*Elvis Perez*" a parody of Elvis Presley. Lalo wrote more than eight-hundred songs including "*Tacos for Two*" a parody of "*Cocktails for Two*" and "*There's No Tortillas*" to the tune of "*O Sole Mio.*" He and 3 high school buddies kicked off their career appearing at the 1933 World Exposition in Chicago. He was seventeen at that time. Lalo recorded for Imperial Records. He had a beautiful rich baritone singing voice that made him a heart throb for many Hispanic women through the 1940s and 50s. Through the 1960s he owned his own night club in Los Angeles called

"*Lalo's*" where he sang with his own big band nightly. Lalo and his band were also frequent performers at Hollywood's famous "*La Bamba Club*" frequented by movie town's "A" listers.

We discovered we had a mutual long-term friend in Colorado who'd frequently, through the years, arranged bookings for Lalo's band. His band annually toured the "Farm Worker Circuit" throughout the Rocky Mountain area and the Southwest.

Several of Lalo's Spanish language songs were featured in the *Luis Valdez* stage musical, later made into a movie "*Zoot Suit*". These were primarily swing band songs labeled "Pachuca Music". Lalo-written songs from that show included "*Vamos A Bailar*" "*Marijuana Boogie*", "*Los Chucos Suaves*" and "*Barrio Viejo*". Late in his life he recorded an album with *Los Lobos* (*Papa Lalo's Magic Balloon*) that was nominated for a Grammy. Members of Los Lobos called Lalo "Papa Lalo." To many Hispanic entertainers Lalo was "*The Father of Chicano Music*".

A man I'd met while traveling with Lalo, Ben Esparza produced Lalo's last CD which featured Lalo singing his songs with a large swing band. To promote that album Lalo would wear a specially designed "Zoot Suit" outfit. At that time Lalo was 83 years old and still performing like a champ.

That same year I was hosting an information booth for CDFA at the National Orange Festival. Lalo was appearing on a stage across the fairgrounds with a swing band performing his Zoot Suit era songs wearing his Zoot Suit costume. During a break he learned I was in the CDFA booth. He, with guitar in hand came over to join me, started signing pictures while at our booth and singing his well known English language satires.

I asked Lalo if he would write a song about the Mediterranean Fruit Fly. The lyrics would explain the farm industry in California was being threatened by this troublesome little fly that may be hiding inside fruit and other products people ship or carry into the U.S. from Mexico. The recording and an accompanying public service announcement was distributed to Spanish language radio stations throughout California. It was played so frequently it actually became very popular. It was called "La Mosca".

Lalo had a reserve of positive energy. We featured him as the Department's Hispanic celebrity spokesman for three more major campaigns including an award-winning project to warn Southern California residents about an infestation of Red Imported Fire ants.

Larry and I took Lalo on a driving trip along the U.S.—Mexican border. We held news conferences at border crossing inspection stations in California, Arizona and Texas, displaying piles of illegal fruit confiscated at the border. Lalo would sing his songs ending with "La Mosca" and his presence always drew media from both sides of the border.

At the start of our journey we slipped just across the border to the edge of Tijuana to make a quick stop at a mobile trailer housing an office of the local Spanish language newspaper. We were greeted by a single young man, about 16 or 17 years old, he saw Lalo and ran out the door and disappeared. We were left standing alone wondering whether we should wait for someone to call or contact the Policia that a teenager may have broken into the empty trailer and fled when we arrived. We waited about 5 minutes and suddenly were joined by a crowd of about 30 people, led by the young man. They all wanted to see Lalo. We did get a nice story out of that unusual visit.

I took Lalo to each of the International Airports in California to serenade and provide brochures to people waiting for flights to Mexico. I took him to predominantly Spanish language grade schools in Los Angeles and in San Diego where he would sing songs and tell stories to children. With the help of my very talented son Troy we used sound clips from Lalo's children's records implying *Las Ardillitas* were talking to Lalo from behind the curtain and were too shy to come out to join him on the stage. The children could hear the characters but couldn't see them. We gave the kids colorful activity books and flyers to take to their parents printed in Spanish and in English warning of the fruit fly threat.

We recorded radio and television announcements featuring Lalo and attended, with Lalo as our draw, a number of Hispanic celebrations and events across the state. One year for Cinco de Mayo, the California Legislature adopted a resolution honoring Lalo's work with our department. Lalo attended that legislative session and sang for the lawmakers.

Lalo lived near Palm Springs and for twenty-five years was a featured singer at a well known Mexican Food Restaurant in Palm Desert. Interestingly one of his biggest fans and a frequent visitor to the restaurant was *Frank Sinatra*. Lalo told me when Sinatra arrived he would watch to gauge "the King's" mood before talking to him or walking over to serenade him (can you imagine serenading Sinatra?) for if he was in a bad mood it was wise not to bother him, but if he was in a good mood you knew it would be a fun evening.

Lalo and I became good friends over the few years we knew one another. He actually flew to our home in Northern California to entertain for my daughter's wedding. My wife and I still laugh when we talk about Lalo at my daughter's wedding. He was sitting at a table while a D-J was playing dance songs. An old 50s rock song came up and my wife, who loves to dance, journeyed onto the dance floor to dance by herself. Suddenly we all hear Lalo's Booming voice shouting "Go Patty Go!" clapping his hands with glee.

Lalo was a close friend of the Ronstadt Family in Arizona. *Linda Ronstadt* said she had many fond childhood memories of being serenaded by Lalo. Linda Ronstadt sang a tribute to Lalo at his funeral. He passed away on March 15, 2005 at an assisted living center in Rancho Mirage. His wife of 34 years Lidia (a delightful and beautiful lady) one of his sons, his daughter Patricia and his Granddaughter Alana were at his side. Lalo was born on Christmas Eve, 1916—he was 88 years old when he died.

Upon his death National Public Broadcasting produced a one hour special television program commemorating his incredible life. He was originally from the Tucson, Arizona area. In 1980 Lalo was officially declared a *National Folk Hero* by the Smithsonian Institute. In 1996 he was presented the *National Medal of the Arts* by *President Bill Clinton* at the White House (In telling me about that special evening he took great delight in the fact he repeatedly danced with Hillary). In 1992 he received the *National Heritage Award from the National Endowment for the Arts*. He loved life, he loved people, especially the ladies and he loved to perform. Wherever Lalo went, be it a meeting or just eating at a restaurant he would end up singing and entertaining.

A number of times he and I had stopped to eat somewhere and when Hispanic workers in the kitchen found out who was there our table would be surrounded and Lalo would pick up his guitar, which he carried with him almost always. I remember picking Lalo up at his home in Cathedral City, near Palm Springs, We were driving to San Diego where he was to make several appearances for our Red Imported Fire

Ant Program. When we reached San Diego, Lalo said he was hungry. We were short on time so I pulled off the Freeway and stopped at the first restaurant we came to. The name of the Restaurant was German but it featured Chinese Food. As we entered I told Lalo, "German restaurant, Chinese food menu no serenading the staff here". However we soon learned the waiters, waitresses, the cooking staff and the management staff were all Hispanic and we were once again the center of all activity. In fact I had to run out to the car to grab Lalo's guitar.

The night of my daughter Katrina's wedding Lalo and I slipped out of the wedding reception and decided to sneak off and get some Mexican food (We hadn't taken time to eat at the reception). As usual when the staff at the restaurant in Yuba City learned of Lalo's presence our table was surrounded and Lalo was performing. In the meantime my daughter Katrina was fuming. She and her new husband were preparing to leave the reception to head for Cancun where they would honeymoon. However all of her clothes were in the trunk of my car.

When I dropped Lalo off at his Motel and returned to the reception I was greeted with a lot of scowls and a lot of tears from my angry frustrated daughter. They still made all their planned connections and I was eventually forgiven.

One year I accompanied Lalo to a Mexican Independence Day Parade and Festival in San Jose. Lalo was to be the Parade Master and was to ride in a convertible waving at the crowd. Early in the morning I called his room to suggest he meet me for breakfast. There was no answer. I went to his room and knocked on his door. No answer. I walked around the hotel and couldn't find him. Lalo was elderly so I started getting concerned, contacted the house detective and told him we should open Lalo's room to be sure he was OK. His room was empty. I went out to the parking lot and spotted him, sitting under a shade tree with two young ladies. He had his guitar and had been serenading them for two hours.

I told him he had to hurry because the convertible driver was to pick him up at a nearby parking lot to get into the parade. I went on to look at the parade but I didn't see Lalo so I went back for a look. He was still standing in the parking lot waiting to be picked up. The convertible driver hadn't waited. I told Lalo "let's quickly walk over to the parade route and see if you could jump on a float or something". He did ending up on a radio station truck, on the bed of the truck with a loud speaker system singing to the crowds which is what he really wanted to do anyway.

The fourteen years I worked at the California Department of Food and Agriculture definitely broadened my understanding of the costly big battles against very small pests. California itself is a laboratory for pests. During my tenure with the department I managed public awareness campaigns on a multitude of problems.

- The gypsy moth destroyed forests as quickly and as devastatingly as forest fires.
- The eucalyptus longhorn borer threatened the very survival of Southern California's large and beautiful eucalyptus trees.
- Africanized bees endangered the lives of anyone nearing its hives.
- Ash Whitefly, never before detected in California virtually infested twenty-one counties in California in August of 1981.

Estimates of the numbers of fruits, vegetables and plants that can be destroyed by the Mediterranean fruit fly go as high as two-hundred-twenty different products. Many of these pests arrived in California in shipments of agricultural products from other countries, and/or in suitcases and bags carried by international travelers arriving in California.

In 1991, shortly after I moved from the Los Angeles Medfly Project to work for the agency in Sacramento, I was assigned to develop and implement a communication plan for the newly created California Airport/Maritime Inspection Program. Most of the funding for this project came from fees imposed on airlines, cargo ship lines and cruise ship lines for required inspection at International ports in California to confiscate fruit shipments believed to be carrying or infested with a wide variety of pests.

We adopted a USDA slogan "Don't Pack a Pest." The USDA increased the number of inspectors at the airports and at the Port of Los Angeles, and we created a program training mixed breed dogs rescued from animal shelters to smell suitcases and packages and notify handlers when they smell fruit. In the first year of the program at Los Angeles International Airport alone there were nearly 18,000 interceptions of regulated fruit, plant and meat products. We placed trained dog teams at postal and UPS facilities to sniff packages. The USDA also created a dog sniffing program using trained Beagles.

We created a team of special investigators in the produce market area of Log Angeles to stop illegal smuggling of fruit, produce, plants, livestock and meat. There were several unbelievable incidents leading to the arrest and prosecution of shippers trying to smuggle exotic products by hiding them beneath unregulated products. We found there was such a black market for exotic fruits that many unmarked trucks parked around the Los Angeles Produce Market were used to lure buyers away from the legitimate markets to tap into the higher economic return illegal exotic fruit business.

The population of immigrants from all over the world in Los Angeles created that demand, and exotic fruits, as a result, brought premium prices. Because well over two-hundred-fifty agricultural commodities were grown and marketed in California these hitchhiking pests created an economic threat that could result in the loss of billions of dollars.

The multi-year Airport Maritime Don't Pack a Pest Campaign had many elements. One of them was quite useful and required a touch of clandestine activity to inaugurate. I'd been told Australian officials had developed a tall wooden structure that was placed at all airports hosting International flights called "amnesty bins." I contacted the Australian Agriculture Department (privately funded by the way) and traced down the creator of this project. He sent me the blueprints for these boxes which are designed to collect quarantined fruits, vegetables and food products giving travelers a last opportunity to get rid of them before risking a fine by getting caught sneaking them on board. I contracted with a Sacramento Cabinet maker to build us four of these structures.

When they were completed we mounted large posters we'd created for our campaign and sent letters to USDA, U.S. Customs, the Immigration Service and the Los Angeles International Airport Board announcing our intention to place them in the International Inspection area. We received no replies. We waited several weeks and still there were no replies. I contacted the Inspectors Supervisor for the USDA-Animal Plant Health Inspection Service Beagle Dog inspection team at LAX. He told me to bring them down—let him know when we arrived and he would let us into the area. One of my co-horts and I picked up a large State truck at one of our CDFA work facilities, loaded the large boxes on the back and made the 9 hour drive to Los Angeles. We parked right outside the entrance to the well-secured International inspection area.

The Supervisor granted us access and we placed all four "amnesty bins" at key locations. We returned wondering aloud how long it would take for a response. Several months later I received a letter from a supervisor at LAX who informed us the colors of the boxes and the posters did not match the color scheme of the airport and he suggested we re-paint them—which we did. After hitting so many brick walls trying to get authorization to place the bins in the terminal, no one really paid much attention once they were in place. The inspector cleaned them out daily and confiscated very large amounts of quarantined fruit—they worked very well. The only problem area involved things left in the bins with the fruit like used epidermis needles, trash, baby diapers etc.

We staffed information booths at the Vietnamese Orange Festival celebrations, Korean Festivals, Thai Festivals at the Buddhist Temples, attended a formal dinner at the home of the Thai Ambassador, held a well attended news conference in China Town, and many Hispanic Cinco De Mayo and September 23rd memorial celebrations. We distributed thousands of balloons, "Don't Pack a Pest" Stickers, Medfly flyswatters and more. We conducted a poll at several festivals and learned most of the 3-thousand respondents had little or no idea there were fruits, vegetables and exotic foods that were quarantined and the fine for violating that quarantine could be as much as $25,000.

I was able to get participation in our education efforts from the fee payers by authorizing a 10% fee discount if airlines would show our "Don't Pack a Pest" cartoon video on all incoming International flights and would allow us to train their staffs on quarantine laws. Cruise ships would receive a fee discount if they would play our videos and distribute our written materials in multiple language. Cargo ship carriers crews would be required to participate in training sessions we would present.

I got the idea for the cartoon story from a video produced by Canada. The cartoon featured a beagle dog inspector in uniform stopping an airline traveler for inspection, another passenger sneaks by him carrying a small bag without being seen by the inspector dog. When the bag carrying passengers walks out of the airport an insect crawls out of the bag. Soon there are thousands of insects eating everything in sight. It was entertaining and because there was no dialogue it reached all, despite language barriers.

When I was a broadcast reporter, as mentioned earlier in this book it was fairly common to find yourself dealing with or connected in some way to murder and mayhem. Unexpectedly even in the somewhat drab world of agriculture I was exposed to murder and mayhem. Making frequent visits to the Los Angeles International Airport I developed a friendship with some of the inspectors. They worked long hours inspecting thousands of bags for quarantined food products, often at odd hours. Scheduling staff for this 24 hour per day 7 day a week effort was at times complex and emotional for those directly involved. I never dreamed I would again be dealing with murder and death issues.

There was one dog handler on the inspection team with an incredible depth of knowledge about a little of everything. He was also very funny and I always enjoyed talking with him. One day in April 1998, he was called to his supervisor's office for a routine scheduling conference. About 10 minutes into the meeting gunfire erupted. My friend, David Rothman had inexplicably pulled out a .380 caliber semiautomatic handgun and shot 44 year old Clayton Ijima and 44 year old Morley Suzuki, his supervisors, then turned the gun on himself. Suzuki was still alive when police arrived but died in the hospital about a half hour after arriving there. Police said thirteen bullets were fired in the altercation. No one is sure what actually caused the incident but if anything it was indicative of the level of stress faced daily in that kind of work.

Even at CDFA we experienced murder and mayhem. 57 year old Bill Shaline, a long time meat inspector for our agency, Jeannie Hillery, grandmother and a federal compliance officer from Alameda, California, and 52 year old Tom Quadros of Hayward where shot to death by the owner of a small sausage factory in San Leandro, California in March of 2000. Two days before the incident Shaline was asked to inspect the sausage plant with another state worker who had gone there earlier and learned the owner, Stuart Alexander had been operating without a license. Alexander wasn't at the plant when the officers arrived. They waited. When he returned and saw the inspectors, there were words exchanged. Alexander walked into his office about 10 feet away, removed a handgun from a cabinet and literally gunned down the three inspectors. Alexander walked outside the building and started chasing a fourth inspector who fled during the shootings. He fired at that inspector, another CDFA officer five times but the inspector was not injured. Alexander gave up the chase, went back into the building and fired additional shots in the head of each of the victims.

Three handguns were found at the scene. Seventeen shell casings from a 9 millimeter and .380 caliber gun were found. Alexander was convicted of the three murders and sentenced to death. Before the sentence was carried out he died in prison of a pulmonary embolism.

It is amazing the numbers and variety of fruits, meats and veggies that are carried around the globe and it's truly amazing there aren't more outbreaks of various types destroying crops. Another of our Airport-Maritime Inspection projects involved a week-long inspection at the Port of Los Angeles. More than three-hundred-fifty cargo shipments (that's some six million pounds of cargo) were inspected. Fifty ships were boarded for galley inspection and garbage handling compliance. The baggage of more than 7-thousand cruise ship passengers was sniffed and/or searched. Nineteen of the cargo shipments contained prohibited commodities. That included citrus peel, pepper corn, okra, red rice, soup mix with meat, and one-thousand year old eggs? The shipments were from China, Ecuador, Hong Kong, Indonesia, Korea, Lebanon, the Philippines, Sri Lanka, Taiwan and Thailand. The cruise ship baggage inspection resulted in one-hundred-seventeen interceptions of quarantined material. This quick spot check provided some perspective in the enormity of the challenge—yet the Airport Maritime Inspection Program died on the vine.

The California Airport Maritime Inspection Service went the way of most good programs that actually accomplish something ending for lack of funds. The program, as mentioned earlier was funded by inspection fees from international carriers, airlines, cargo ships, cruise lines all of whom fought the fee through the court system. When the issue lost before a California Court judge the program was ended.

I had three major challenges remaining during my tenure with the State. An outbreak of Karnal Bunt disease in wheat, Red Imported Fire Ants threatening city folk and farm workers in several areas of the state and the Exotic Newcastle Disease fight devastating birds in Southern California.

In 1996 I was selected to return to the Imperial Valley (remember Brawley?) to serve as the media spokesman for a new emergency project resulting from an infestation of Karnal Bunt disease in wheat. The project headquarters was at the Imperial County Fairgrounds between

Brawley and El Centro, California. It was summer, harvest time for wheat and extremely hot. I also decided to document the entire project on video so everywhere I went; a very large very heavy video camera and tripod came with me.

At that time housing in the area was limited at best. There were motels but most were old and hot. I was lucky and made a deal for a room at the Barbara Worth Country Club at nearby Holtville, California. I was on that project for about three months and the setting surrounded by very old oak trees and a golf course, and a nice bar and restaurant made this tour acceptable.

Another irony, several years later I needed work done on my home computer. We were living in Colorado again at that time. The computer repairman that came to our house was a member of the family that owns and operates the Barbara Worth Country Club in Holtville, a small world indeed.

Karnal Bunt is a fungal disease of wheat, durum wheat and triticale. The fungus invades the wheat kernels and gets its nutrition from the endosperm (a nutrient tissue surrounding the seeds of flowering plants.) The fungus makes the wheat smell bad and the bunted kernels can't be used in flour. The disease was first identified in 1931 in the Indian state of Haryana in which there is a district called Karnal. It spread to wheat in Iraq, Afghanistan, Pakistan and Nepal then in the 1960s it was discovered in Mexico. In 1996 it was found in California, Arizona, New Mexico and Texas. The seriousness of the outbreak was demonstrated clearly when foreign markets refused to import any wheat from infected regions. Although infected wheat is not dangerous to eat it does leave the wheat in an unpleasant and unpalatable state.

The disease was carried from one field to another through contaminated seed or on farm equipment; however it was also possible wind could carry the viral spores through the air for short distances. Wheat harvesters were required to completely wash down before being allowed to be used in other fields. There was a lot of wheat to be inspected. An emergency quarantine on the movement of wheat was imposed requiring inspection and certification before any wheat could be moved out of the infested area.

Fields within the regulated area were sampled at harvest time. If the samples were negative for Karnal Bunt, the wheat could be cut and delivered in the grain market. If samples were found to be positive, the grain could be cut but had to be moved to a USDA approved storage area until final disposal. Interstate movement of "regulated articles" required a special USDA permit. There were a number of somewhat boisterous meetings between government officials and angered farmers. The most serious effect of the infestation was quarantines imposed by foreign countries who didn't want to risk spread of the disease to their area. There were quarantines imposed by seventy different countries. The fungus can survive in the soil for 5 years or more. The development of Karnal bunt-resistant winter wheat varieties has been difficult in the United States. The project in the end was successful and it was another great learning experience although much simpler than the high profile Medfly emergency in terms of providing media information.

Probably my biggest frustration was the fact that although I was way down in the no-man's country again I forgot to retrieve my children's gas motor powered pickup truck and my big box of reel-to-reel celebrity interview tapes. Maybe next time?

My next major crisis campaign involved the discovery in Southern California of a long-time Southern U.S. pest the Red Imported Fire Ant (RIFA). I was to coordinate a lengthy and expensive Public Relations Campaign to alert residents of infested areas about the dangers posed by this pest and attempt to develop a two-way communication to help us trace where and when the infestation was moving. For the third time we contracted with Fleishman Hillard Public Relations. My first campaign working with Fleishman Hillard, "Don't Pack a Pest" won the Agency the coveted *"Silver Anvil"* award from the Public Relations Society of America.

That involved our Spanish language outreach with Lalo Guerrero. This Red Imported Fire Ant campaign resulted in our agency's second Silver Anvil, selected as the best of several hundred entrees from throughout the nation. As one of the developers and implementers I was proud of this program.

It actually started in 1998 when there were some serious incidents of stinging in Orange County. The Red Imported Fire Ant stings repeatedly and painfully. If a person gets too near the ants' mound thousands of ants immediately swarm up the leg of the intruder stinging all the way. In some cases the ant stings can be fatal. These ants have been known to kill small birds and animals and destroy some crops. It was later found in Los Angeles, Riverside, San Bernardino, San Diego, Fresno, Stanislaus,

Madera and Merced Counties. The threatening ant mounds were even found on the playground of a grade school in Orange County.

The campaign itself has been described by some experts as the "picture perfect model" of how a public affairs education campaign should be implemented. In fact one well known Southern California University Professor broke down the elements of the campaign to use in his classroom and also included those comments in a textbook he developed for Public Relations Courses at the University.

We kicked off the campaign with a very well attended news conference which allowed reporters and photographers access to get close shots of ant colonies, close-up video of the live ants themselves, sting victims were interviewed, researchers were present to answer technical questions, our celebrity spokespersons, *Paul James*, host of the HGTV show *"Gardening by the Yard,"* and for the Spanish speaking Lalo Guerrero also participated in the news conference. To give you an idea how effective our news conference was there was a total of fifty-eight minutes of air time devoted to coverage of that event. Call volumes to the hotline jumped as much as four-hundred per cent after each media exposure and/or event. Bill inserts containing RIFA information and newsletters combined reached an estimated eleven million people. With the participation and support of Los Angeles PBS Television personality *Hewer Howser* we recorded television announcements and informational videos. Howser actually lived in the Palm Springs area and feared that he may have found Red Imported Fire Ant mounds in his own backyard (If I remember correctly his ants fortunately weren't fire ants). He did an entire program about the problem for Public television. We developed an online computer game and school projects distributed with the help of *"Ag in the Classroom"*—reaching students in 5-thousand schools.

We included RIFA information in billing mailings to utility customers in all the infested areas, put together information binders for all county officials, hosted "neighborhood Watch-Out Meetings" and we developed, at the midway point, a specially targeted campaign addressing agricultural producers and farm workers in the San Joaquin Valley. That occurred when huge ant mounds were found in almond and fruit tree orchards in the Central valley. We learned many farm workers had been attacked by the ants but the workers were reluctant to notify the land owners. We created RIFA safety kits for farm workers, partnered with several agricultural groups to distribute RIFA information, held a series of news conferences in orchards displaying the huge ant mounds and did a number of radio and television interviews on agricultural programs.

A post survey of RIFA awareness indicated overall public awareness of the pest increased 349 per cent when compare to the baseline survey results. The entire campaign was exhausting but exciting. For my part I would say my role in coordinating, monitoring and serving as the primary liaison between Fleishman Hillard and CDFA was another career highlight. It was exhausting but I feel good about the entire episode.

The next crisis mode situation in which I was involved had to do with birds. All kinds of birds again focused in the enormous Los Angeles area. I was selected to respond to media inquiries on a joint Federal-State Project to eradicate an outbreak of Exotic Newcastle Disease. To get an idea of the scope of this project here is a list of the agencies participating:

- USDA-Animal Plant Health Inspection Service,
- Agricultural Research Service,
- California Department of Food and Agriculture,
- California Department of Forestry and Fire Protection,
- The Grain Inspection, Packers and Stockyards Administration,
- California Office of Emergency Services
- U.S. Forest Service.

This project sent me to Los Angeles again for several weeks. The project lasted 11 months and involved up to 7000 workers from the participating agencies. Approximately 3 + million birds were destroyed to prevent the disease from spreading. It did spread to a few large poultry and egg operations requiring many of their birds to be killed although we were instructed not to use terms like "killed" or "destroyed"—the proper term was "depopulated". Once again our project became a big news story in Los Angeles.

Our veterinarians were actually going house to house checking people's pet birds and backyard birds or chicken flocks. The number of chickens in many of the backyards in Los Angeles was enormous. In El Monte, several families would purchase chickens and keep them in one centrally located large backyard, kind of a neighborhood "commune" for chickens. Several residents had large collections of exotic birds. A number of the residents had fighting roosters that had values estimated in the thousands of dollars. It was not legal to fight the birds but was not illegal to raise and own the fighting birds.

As the media contact for the project I had to deal with all kinds of rumors and wild stories, some of them were true most were either highly exaggerated or simply untrue. People in the area were very emotional about their birds. We again called on Lalo Guerrero to help us get the message out.

In another incident getting a lot of media play, one of the project's veterinarians, visiting a private residence killed the family's pet bird on the spot in front of the children. That vet was dismissed from the project and sent home and sensitivity training became mandatory for all workers in the project. Despite a number of highly charged, emotion filled and angry community meetings the program was successful in keeping the disease from spreading, saving millions of birds around the country.

When the project ended, I was appointed to serve as the State of California representative with the USDA team for an in-depth after-review of the project. Our task was to evaluate all of the many complex elements of the project and make recommendations identifying problems and how better to address those issues should there be another emergency project of that size and scope.

An After-Review Team Afterthought— The Civil War Experience

The after-review team met at a government facility in Virginia to draft our final report. When we finished we discovered we had several hours before we were to fly back home. We rented a car and took a relatively short drive to Gettysburg, Pennsylvania, the site of the bloodiest battle of the Civil War. The reason I bring this up is the eerie feeling I had as we travelled through that historic battlefield. Talk about mental mind pictures. More than 50-thousand American men, many barely out of their teens were killed or injured in that place over a three day period. Confederate casualties, dead, wounded and missing totaled

28,000—Union casualties 23,000. It was considered the "turning point battle" of the civil war.

Wandering through the fields of the Gettysburg National Park grounds brings some reality to what happened at that place. It is mind boggling in fact. At least 75,000 confederate men and 88,000 union soldiers fought in that three day battle. What is somewhat startling to me is the indescribable uninvited sensitivity one feels at that place.

Even if you were totally uneducated and carefree you would sense that something really horrible had occurred there. The scene, when we were there, was extremely quiet, with a slight breeze—we seemed to be the only visitors present at that particular time. I've read about the civil war battles—I've seen movies about the battle but the reality doesn't impact you unless you are standing where it really happened. Even visiting the house where President Lincoln wrote his infamous Gettysburg Address is a surreal experience. The battle was fought July 1 through July 3 in 1863. On November 19th of that year Lincoln visited that battlefield to help dedicate the field as a military cemetery.

Edward Everett of Massachusetts was the primary speaker that day. His address lasted two hours. Lincoln's Gettysburg address lasted just two minutes and is praised to this day as one of the best speeches ever delivered. The words he used "government of the people, by the people, and for the people" today still define democracy. That short visit on that day affirmed my belief in spirits. The spirits you sense on that battlefield are indeed surreal.

Another Diversion

Devoting as much time as I did to work that required me to go to Southern California I was afforded the opportunity to become better acquainted with my oldest son Troy and his wife Janet. Troy started working when he was but fifteen as a disc jockey at the local skating Rink in Yuba City, CA and at a neighborhood nightclub. After he and Janet were married they moved to the Los Angeles area where Troy enrolled in a training program for audio engineers, the people that record and mix live music for record production and for live performances. Janet was a good singer and got a job selling Karaoke equipment at a specialty store in Santa Monica.

They started going to bars that featured Karaoke. Troy would often tweak up the bar's sound systems and Janet would sing. She became a local favorite in several of the clubs. I would often tag along with them and the experiences got more and more interesting. You start seeing the same people at every Karaoke bar you visit. Each singer has a "signature" song and it is considered unacceptable for anyone to sing someone else's song. Karaoke can be painful to listen to, but in Los Angeles there are enough almost-professional singers who are still waiting tables hoping to be discovered, or off-duty show people just singing to have a good time that these events can be most entertaining.

There was, for example a 50s something gentleman who always dressed to the hilt and sang only the songs of Billy Eckstine (I know Elizabeth "Who's Billy Eckstine?") who was considered the first romantic black male in popular music. This Eckstine sound alike also had a popular radio program featuring several members of this "in" group of Karaoke singers.

When my daughter-in-law was recorded one night singing *"Blues in the Night"* and he played the recording on his radio program it was an indicator she was an accepted foe in the strange world of Karaoke. Janet participated and won in a sponsored competition. Each Karaoke bar in California would run a singing contest and the winner would advance to a state final, then onto a regional final. Janet won at the Burbank Bicycle Club where the state competition was also held. I happened to be in town the night of the State/Regional finals. The house was packed. Singers and their supporters were there from all over the state, Washington and Oregon. Each singer could sing two songs. Janet sang *"Bewitched"* and *"Blues in the Night"* and won first place. There was almost a street brawl in front of the club because two of the competitors were planning to sing the same song.

One evening we decided to visit a hotel located near the Port of Los Angeles where one of the frequent Karaoke singers was hosting the performances after winning that bar's competition. We enjoyed the show, and then stayed until closing talking with her. I'd rented a new Buick. We headed back up the 405 Freeway to return to Burbank when Troy told us he had to use a restroom. At the next exit I pulled off the Freeway looking for a place he could relieve himself. Looking around we saw men standing around trash barrels in which fires were set to keep them warm. We were in Compton, where there'd been some bitter rioting.

I finally pulled into an alley, before Troy could get out of the car a police cruiser pulled in behind us. I explained the situation to the officer who told us to follow him to the police station. When we arrived there he told Troy to use the rest room at the station. Troy said there were a strange collection of characters in the station. When he returned to the car, the officer came around to my window. He said "Please follow me to the freeway. We need to get you folks out of here as quickly as we can." He really wasn't concerned we might have been drinking, he just wanted to make sure we didn't get robbed or have the car hijacked. When we got back on 405 North again Janet suddenly blurted out "Oh my gosh! It just dawned on me why the police escorted us out of town!"

One of my most humiliating moments occurred during one of these Karaoke evenings in Los Angeles. My daughter-in-law had been urging me to join in as a singer. I repeatedly told her I am not a singer but she persisted and I finally gave in. I selected as my song "Moon Dance" written by Van Morrison For a solid week before my big night I practiced my song (mostly while driving my car). When the weekend arrived I went to los Angeles and checked into a motel. I was practicing my song in my room (in my underwear) in front of a mirror when the maid walked into the room. We were both embarrassed. When the time arrived, I bravely strutted up on the stage and started singing.

I simply could not project. I sang on key, remembered the words, established great eye contact but couldn't sing loud enough to be heard above a whisper, even with the microphone and an amplification system. My daughter-in-law and her friend, who was the hostess for the evening, attempted to bail me out by grabbing a toy saxophone and a toy trumpet and pretended to play them as they danced. Still the crowd politely applauded. The hostess remarked "Boy—you are a soooofffft singer!" That was my first and last effort at becoming a karaoke star.

Around the year 2002 I was diagnosed with Muscular Dystrophy. This was indeed a shock to me. I'd spent a good deal of my time while working for the State of California packing and unpacking, constructing and tearing down complex displays for the Food and Agriculture Department for Fairs around the state. One display was contained in twelve large cases, each weighing around 80 pounds. I was pretty good at transporting those cases, sometimes for a distance of up to three-quarters of a mile.

One of my children, my surrogate daughter Lisa (I explain later) and her husband Matt had moved to Maryland where he attended the Uniform Services University of Health Care at Bethesda and received his Doctorate. During that time Lisa worked as an investigator for the Department of Defense. During our visit, while walking across a very large parking lot at a shopping mall, I developed a pain in my right calf.

When we returned home I went to our doctor in Yuba City, California. He said it might be arthritis or perhaps an Achilles tendon problem but to be certain he sent me to a neurologist. The neurologist was young (about 12 I think), Chinese and difficult to understand. His name was Chan Han. He hooked up a gadget that told him it wasn't a problem with my nervous system, in fact he said (I think he said) my nervous system was in excellent condition, more responsive than for men much younger than I. He then hooked up another machine and concluded "Something's happening with muscles". I scheduled a day to have a small piece of my right calf muscle removed and sent to a laboratory for analysis. About 3 weeks later I was informed the diagnosis was Muscular Dystrophy but the type was uncertain. Because of that uncertainty the muscle sample was forwarded from the University of California at Davis to the Stanford University Medical Laboratory. They confirmed it was MD but they couldn't really decide what type. I was then asked to go to the University of California Medical Center in San Francisco to see a Neurologist there. He confirmed I had MD but he wanted to send the sample to a laboratory in Washington D.C. for analysis but my insurance company refused to pay for any more analysis. He did know my disease was genetic. I received it from my mother (females are usually the carrier) and it was progressive but he didn't know if or when it would stop progressing. He also knew he could not treat the disease.

I continued to work for the State of California for about two more years. Although I was certainly old enough to qualify for retirement I chose to apply for a disability retirement (that makes insurance much less costly with the state.) It took about one year to get my disability approved, even though I could no longer walk or easily dress myself for it had spread up my legs, my wrists and hands and arms.

Still, I was immediately offered a job with the United States Department of Agriculture, Animal and Plant Health Inspection Service. I knew most of those folks in California and my friend Larry of "Larry and Larry" gave me a decisive recommendation. I was to fill-in for a Public Affairs Officer who worked in the Agency's Western Region (the 22 Western States) located in Fort Collins, Colorado, only about fifteen miles from my home town, Greeley. She was an officer in the Wyoming Army National Guard and her Unit had been called to active duty in Iraq. The term of the job was to be from 1 to 4 years. I stayed at that job for 4 years, although she returned to work in nine months. During that 4 year period I travelled frequently making at least 6 trips to Washington D.C. and I was frequently called on short notice to fly somewhere the next day for a variety of reasons including:

- Helping representatives of Federal agencies in Washington State prepare for emergency programs, like "Bird flu" and develop a method of communicating with one another to coordinate information during an emergency.
- Helping with media and serving as a moderator for a panel discussion at the Chicago Mercantile Exchange regarding the trade and market impacts of Mad Cow Disease in the United States.
- Serving as the on-site media contact in Austin, Texas when Mad Cow Disease was confirmed on one area ranch.
- Helping staff a booth promoting the "National Animal I-D system" at the National Pork Exposition in Iowa.
- Helping develop a training program for 4H youngsters on the "National Animal I-D plan" in Indianapolis
- Meeting with officials of a large egg and poultry facility in Iowa about the emergency plan should bird flu break-out.
- Scheduling an early morning news conference at the National Association of Farm Broadcasters annual meeting in Kansas City.
- Hosting an information booth at the American Royal Livestock show in Kansas City three years in a row.
- With Larry hosting booths at the National Western Livestock Show in Denver, promoting "National Animal ID"

- Hosting an information booth on "National Animal ID" in Fort Worth, Texas—Southwest Stockgrowers conference
- Hosting an information booth for three consecutive years at the Northern International Livestock Exhibition in Billings, Montana.
- Discussing "Mad Cow Disease" at the Wyoming State Fair Ranchers Meeting
- Hosting an information booth at the Kansas State Fair in Salina, Kansas
- Helping escort a reporter for Newsweek Magazine through the National Veterinary Services Laboratory in Iowa.

For nearly 20 years, this old DJ-Reporter focused on emergency agricultural crisis. A far cry from Greeley's Friday night teen dances. It was difficult to travel however the Agency helped pay for rented mobility scooters at each site providing the mobility I needed.

When that four year term ended I started again sending out applications. One Sunday evening I received a phone call from the Montana State Conservationist for the United States Department of Agriculture, Dave White. Federal job interviews are usually stuffy affairs during which a panel of Federal employees asks you a number of annoying questions "Where do you hope to be 10 years from now?" (Still alive?) "Why do you want to work for us?" (Money) "What are your weaknesses?" (Which muscle to you want to start with?) Mr. White told me he'd talked to the folks at APHIS (United States Department of Agriculture. Animal and Plant Health Inspection Service) and they told him I was a good pick. White said "I just need someone who can find his butt with both hands? Can you do that?"(actually I can't—my hands and arms don't allow me to put my arms behind me) I assured him I could although the Muscular Dystrophy impeded my ability to reach behind me. I was offered the job. We moved to Bozeman, Montana.

White later became the "Chief" of the entire National Agency working in Washington D-C and managing the 12-thousand employees around the nation. The Natural Resources Conservation Service (NRCS) is a far different duty than was the Animal and Plant Health Inspection Service (APHIS). APHIS is a regulatory agency with an ultimate goal of keeping the Nations livestock healthy and the Plant industry pest-free.

To accomplish those goals requires the agency to make very unpopular but necessary decisions. Many producers have, at one time or another been very angry at some of those decisions. NRCS on the other hand provides technical expertise and more importantly cost-sharing for producers who elect to implement conservation practices. NRCS is essentially the old Soil Conservation Service, an agency that grew out of the Dust Bowls of the 1930s. It's a much "friendlier" situation.

On Memorial Day 2011 I gave in and retired. I've spent these retirement days developing this document and an audio version for my off-spring's benefit and for friends who always expressed an interest in hearing about my unusual, unusually long and sometimes interesting career.

Chapter Six

What Really Counts

Patricia

As I write this my dear wife Patricia and I are celebrating 45 years together. I can't think of anyone I would rather be with than Pat. She is dyslexic, has trouble spelling, talks at times incessantly and doesn't always hear what is said correctly. But she is good to the core. She's always been loyal and loving. She was and is a terrific mother. She's always accepted her limitations with a shrug. Pat is someone who is who she is and she never pretends to be anyone else which I see as a great trait in any human. She has a short temper at times but returns to normal very quickly. She has unending energy and you can't damage her spirit no matter how hard you try. She tends to blurt out whatever is on her mind, be it a personal issue or an emotional dissertation about gun control. There is little doubt how she is feeling at any given time physically, emotionally or about a given subject. There is no subterfuge with Pat. Strangers, who are usually too quick to judge others often give her very strange looks. If she feels you shouldn't, for example, eat salt because it's unhealthy, she will fill the salt bottle with a substitute and never tell you. She may hide candy from the little girl next door because she feels that person is consuming unhealthy amounts.

All this yet she has an innocence of purpose that is lovable. She still calls movies "shows" she is addicted to television movies that are black and white and produced as long as 70 to 80 years ago but if a modern film or video is being watched and certain foul words are used or there is an abundance of nudity or sex she leaves the room after approximately two minutes. She hates dirty dishes and washes them immediately, likewise dirty clothing must be washed, dried and put away almost as soon as they are removed.

When she makes her weekly visit to the grocery store it is a two-hour journey, reading the labels of everything she considers buying, yet somehow always forgetting what she went to the store to get requiring a return at a later date to get whatever it was, if she remembers. If something upsets her she will blame her obvious displeasure on something that is completely unrelated to what she was angry about. She is my soul mate indeed. She loves to dance and loves to play slot machines.

Unlike me she has a penchant for winning. In my mind she is a winner and if by some miracle I was to again become a twenty-something, knowing what I now know I would marry her all over again.

Troy, Janet and Christopher

Troy Thomas Cooper was a holy terror in High School but has an IQ level much higher than his bravado reading (if there's a way to measure that by number). Since his early childhood he's been one to teach himself the "how" of almost anything (including and especially modern electronics). The work he does is highly technical and requires a continuous learning curve but he makes it appear easy. When computers were still a strange phenomenon to most of us (when Troy was about 12) he was teaching classes for older adults on how to operate a computer. Troy was born in the Denver suburb Englewood.

He's handsome although he's always been very self conscious and shy. I recall a day I visited his High School and he was so fearful that walking around campus with his Dad would appear to be "un-cool" to his classmates, he made an almost comical effort not to walk near me, but keep a distance so it wouldn't look like he was with some strange older "person". When he was still in grade school he was carrying around portable cassette tape machines mixing songs for girls in the neighborhood. He's already taught now 9 year old Christopher to mix and DJ. When he was 14 he started learning how to mix at a local bar where a professional disc jockey, a few years older than Troy, taught him all the tricks. Troy has passed 40 now and isn't as anxious to mix music in clubs but his 9 year old son has his own players and a mixer board and is already taking up his Dad's call.

Troy's worked hard, displayed a lot of skills and has remained working for the same company, Muzak Corporation in Charlotte, North Carolina for around 15 years, as has his bride Janet who showed up at our house when she was still a teenager sleeping on our living room floor claiming she'd been kicked out of her home. She and Troy met when he was the disc jockey for a dance at the local Moose Lodge in Yuba City, California. Janet is a very talented singer (as I mentioned in the "Karaoke" section). She's survived well and provided Troy a wonderful son (and me a Grandson)named Christopher.

Travis

Travis was born in Missoula Montana. He's now in his late 30s. He always seemed to be the smallest kid in his class through grade school, middle school and high school. Perhaps for that reason he always made sure his circle of buddies were at least one to two feet taller than he was. He started working when he was about 13 as a bus boy at restaurants, and later at restaurants as a waiter or cook. He's presently residing in Reno, Nevada.

The Daughter

The baby of our family was a girl we named "Katrina." She however never liked being called "Katrina" so she has informed most of the people in her life as far as she's concerned she is "Tina". She has always worked hard, is very intelligent and highly skilled. She's learned from her long-term boyfriend how to spin fire and the couple is often hired to do that at weddings, parties, even entertaining theater goers on Broadway waiting for the doors to open. She too is a great singer but doesn't want to take it all that seriously.

She graduated from the Seattle Art Institute as an audio engineer.

When she tired of her job with Muzak and later as a commission sales person for the *Guitar Store*, she joined friends to purchase a bus that they converted to a kind of homemade Recreational Vehicle. They took jobs at and followed Renaissance Fairs to several parts of the nation from Texas to Colorado to New York State. She met her boyfriend James in Texas. She and James have been together for at least 8 or 9 years, both are now working for a company that imports neoprene type bags produced in China and both are doing well living in Montgomery New York. She is the Inventory Manager for a corporation called "Built". I am very proud of my daughter who" hangs in there. "I have faith she can tackle any problem that comes along. I know this, whatever the challenge she will meet it head-on dealing with it with vigorous independence.

Lisa and Matt—Emma and Ethan

One day Travis and Tina brought a friend home with them from grade school. She was waiting for her mother to pick her up. She was about 10 or 11 years old and the first time I met her she was decked out in a Karate costume. She informed me she was going to learn to do Karate then she did a couple of kicks and we had what seemed to me to be a very adult conversation. This little girl was obviously extremely intelligent and through the years she became a part of our family.

Lisa also spent a good deal of time with us. When she was a junior in High School she started dating a young man who was the captain of the football team and in fact was the class Valedictorian at graduation time. Lisa was also an excellent student and at the time was a cheer leader. They attended the same high school at which I taught broadcasting classes.

Because of her fierce intelligence she and I would get into lengthy and heated debates about all kinds of social issues. She moved in with us after graduating from High School to attend the Junior College while her boy friend Matt attended his first year at the University of California at Davis. Completing Junior College with honors Lisa was accepted at UC Davis and was awarded enough scholarship and Pell Grant money to complete her degree at Davis. She and Matt lived together while they completed their bachelor degrees. Pat and I would frequently visit them in Davis and often joined them on driving trips around California.

It was obvious to us they were soul mates and we often planned sly maneuvers to convince Matt he should suggest they get married. We once planned to take them to San Francisco to the musical "Phantom of the Opera". I hinted to Mat that might be a "cool" time to pop the question, during the intermission at "The Phantom of the Opera". As we approached intermission time, I kept looking at Matt and grinning. Intermission time came, Matt looked at me and smiled, asked if he could get any of us a drink, came back with the drinks (I'm thinking I'll bet he slipped the engagement ring in her drink) she drank the drink. Matt sat down and kept looking at me and smiling. (OK—I'm saying to myself_ he's going to wait until just before the house lights go down and quickly slip the ring on her finger, I thought now that's a cool move.) The lights dim.

Matt reaches over and takes her hand. I stretch to see if he's slipping her the ring. The lights go down and the play resumes. I look at him, he shrugs. As we walked back to the parking lot Pat strikes up a conversation with Lisa and I softly ask Matt "What Happened?" "Awe—I think it would be easier to do it when we're alone not surrounded by hundreds of other people." Well we tried. By the way it was a great show—the one on the stage I mean.

When Matt and Lisa both graduated together they did decide to get married. They had a beautiful ceremony. I had a friend in Sacramento that led an 18 piece dance band and allowed me to pay him a little at a time during the months leading up to the wedding. Matt and Lisa actually took some ballroom dancing lessons to prepare. We had a string quartet from the University, the ceiling at the meeting hall of the Elks Lodge in Marysville was covered with mini Christmas Lights we rounded up about many used to dress about fifteen phony trees. All in all it was a classy affair.

Matt and Lisa have a boy and a girl now. Matt is an Army Major, a Doctor, at this time at the Eisenhower Medical Center in Georgia. He's seen action in both Iraq and Afghanistan. Lisa is devoting herself to be a great mother and housewife.

The Dellwos

Due to the progression of muscular dystrophy I found myself suddenly unable to move the gear shift or safely turn the wheel of my car.

For the first time there was no way around the problem. I could no longer drive a car. I mentioned my plight to a fellow worker at the NRCS office in Bozeman, Dennis Dellwo. I offered what I could in terms of providing some extra income. Dennis called his 26 year old daughter Elizabeth who said she would be interested in helping. She worked a block away from my office. She made an appointment to come to the house to meet us. She was not only one of the prettiest girls I've met but the sweetest.

She invited us to join her family for Christmas Eve services at her Church. She arranged a couple of dinners at our house to meet her family. We really hadn't had much time to meet others and Elizabeth taking us under her wing meant a lot.

A Life Well Spent

I've lived longer than any other male in my family, with the exception of my "Last Real Cowboy" Uncle John on my Mom's side. At this writing he is in his 90s and occasionally still rides his horses.

My Grandmother Cooper lived with dignity, intelligence and beauty until she passed at the age of 105. She outlived all five of her children. I've always regretted not taking the time with her to record interviews and pick her awesome intelligence about her survival and her life. She was eloquent in her speech, her dress and her mannerisms. She lost her husband shortly after I was born and never remarried nor dated anyone else. She was the first woman in Kansas elected to serve on a school board. A position she held for 16 years. She made extra money working as a librarian and whenever she had a break she would read. When I would go to her room to wish her good night at Red Crags she was always engrossed in a book. I grew up in awe of her. I never saw her angry, never heard her utter a bad word, in fact on her side of the family controlling emotions was a requirement.

In her lifetime she'd seen development of cars and airplanes. radio and television, an overwhelming list of developments and changes, to which she consistently adapted. My mother once told me she was puzzled because my Dad's side of the family never hugged or even kissed-on-the-cheek, they simply did not display emotion.

Now that I'm approaching old age, a place I thought I would never be, I think a lot about Grandmother Cooper and my relatives and wonder what she really believed, what she truly felt. I'll never know and perhaps I shouldn't. But as with many things I find perplexing at this age, I'll probably never know whether I am missing an awareness of something about my heritage I shouldn't, or if that thought is simply a figment of my own imagination. I regret my own children have little more than a passing interest in their connections to my family's heritage, for when they do have time to contemplate, the lineage will be forgotten.

These are the people who mean the most to me. There are many in my life that I'll never forget. I believe the longer you live the more aware you become of how ignorant you become but it is an ignorance of self awareness tempered by living. It's difficult to explain to younger friends, the internal frustration one feels knowing the experiences and lessons of a long life, while inadvertently slipping into that arena of self doubt fanned by others defenses, absence of respect and flash judgments. But then again those concerns are frequently the product of your own old over-worked imagination. They can be nothing more than a misperception. The only certainty is I've been fortunate.

Final Thought

I've never been wealthy but I've done the best job I could no matter what the challenge. I've experienced love and comfort. I don't have the terrible kinds of self demons my middle son must fight, for that I thank God. I feel rewarded by a sometimes fascinating and exciting career, yet wonder how it all flew by so quickly. As time moves on and leaves you behind it is difficult in your mind's eye to believe you've grown old with it and must face the reality of death sooner than you want, no matter your age.

When all is said and done it is not the murder, mayhem, memories or even music that remain it is the people who love you, the friends and acquaintances who respect you that count the most.